Tour Aotearoa
A BIKER'S TALE

John Hellemans

mower

A catalogue record for this book is available from the National Library of New Zealand

ISBN 978-1-990003-12-7

A Mower Book
Published in 2021 by Upstart Press Ltd
Level 6, BDO Tower, 19–21 Como St, Takapuna 0622
Auckland, New Zealand

Design by CVD Limited
Printed by Everbest Printing Co. Ltd., China

Front cover: The author at Stirling Point, 3 kms south of Bluff, and the official end of the Tour.
Back cover: 'Huddy' hoofing it down Ninety Mile Beach.
Inside cover maps courtesy Kennett Brothers.

Tour Aotearoa
A BIKER'S TALE

Don't hope that events will turn out the way you want, welcome events in whichever way they happen: this is the path to peace.
—Epictatus

For all my friends

CONTENTS

FOREWORD

When John first suggested I ride the Tour Aotearoa with him, I thought he was joking. John is a superb athlete. His courage and determination in the field of triathlon has won him many awards and accolades. Surely a slowcoach like me would hold up his progress on this long and testing ride? But John was persuasive; I was flattered, and agreed.

In the months prior to the Tour, we undertook a series of training rides. It made us realise what we were going to be in for. Neither of us had second thoughts, although I sensed that John's enthusiasm was diminishing.

We duly started the Tour Aotearoa in late February 2018, and after the first day's riding, just as I was drifting off into an exhausted sleep in our cabin at the Ahipara Holiday Park, I heard the noise of typing from the bunk above me. 'What are you doing? Did you bring your computer?' I asked incredulously. 'Yes,' said John, 'I am keeping a diary.'

The Tour turned out very differently for me than expected and John found himself to be on his own for most of the journey. He is a multi-talented individual. Besides being a skilled and dedicated doctor, and a loving husband, father and grandfather, he is an internationally renowned athlete who is fearless and resolute. These latter traits were to serve him well through the long days and unseasonal weather he encountered en route. I saw a glimpse of this resolve on the day John cycled from Haast to Wānaka in torrential rain. As he biked past me up the steepest section of the Haast Pass, he yelled out, with a look of determination on his face, 'Life! First you suffer, then you die.' His courage and perseverance was again tested two days later when he rode through the uninhabited country of the Von Valley into a southerly storm dishing up ice-cold winds, sleet and snow. Failure to keep cycling through this unseasonal weather could have easily led to his demise.

His wit and self-deprecating humour kept me amused on the ride and has resulted in an entertaining and original story that will appeal to a wider public. I hope you enjoy reading the book as much as I did.

John Hudson

PREFACE

New Zealanders have an uncanny ability to endure hardship and adversity. It is no coincidence that a Kiwi was the first to reach the summit of Mount Everest. Sir Edmund Hillary's attitude of toughness combined with modesty, good manners, a sense of fair play, a degree of stoicism and, above all, a sense of humour embodies the Kiwi spirit of the can-do attitude and the number 8 wire mentality. Because of these prevailing characteristics, New Zealand soldiers were popular and respected among the Allied forces during the First and Second World Wars. It is ingrained in the New Zealand pioneering culture and filters through to how Kiwis play their sport. This is exemplified by the mighty All Blacks, the country's national rugby team and one of the most successful sporting teams in the world. They lead the successes of a proud sporting nation.

The ability to tolerate discomfort is one reason why the physical game of rugby suits the Kiwi spirit. Endurance sports fall into a similar category. Over the years, New Zealand has produced some of the world's best endurance and adventure athletes. These athletes combine the sporting psyche of toughness and passion with a love for the outdoors. Every Kiwi grows up close to nature. While most visitors are intimidated by New Zealand's vast wilderness, Kiwis embrace it. They can't get away from it. Formal and informal outdoor education is a big part of life's curriculum for most young New Zealanders. Junior athletes I have coached over the years turn up in shorts and T-shirts for their mid-winter run and bike training sessions, wondering about the fuss I make with my repeated request to please dress up warm. My grandkids prefer to go places barefoot, wherever and whenever they can. It will be interesting to see how long these special characteristics of the New Zealand spirit will survive in today's global world.

Having grown up in the Netherlands, where every nook and cranny of the country is cultivated and put to good use, I have no such background. When I first arrived in New Zealand in 1978 and observed how sport was played – uncompromising and with a zealous passion of religious proportions – I remember thinking, 'Oh, so that's how you do it.' I applied the 'Kiwi way' to my own sporting endeavours and results came surprisingly quickly. As a consequence, I had a solid career as an athlete in triathlon in my adopted country before turning my energy to coaching.

I wanted to learn more about what made Kiwi athletes tick. I had learned to accept the pain that comes with redlining for a couple of hours. *Redlining* is the term used for driving a car (engine) at or above its rated maximum revolutions per minute, ready to blow up at any time. In sport it refers to going at a pace that you know is at or just above the maximum pace you can sustain for the duration of the race. You stretch your cardiovascular, physiological and muscular systems to the max and beyond. Redlining is painful. Your lungs feel ready to burst and your muscles are screaming to the extent that you want to lie down and cry, but you don't, as you have chosen to do this, you have prepared for it and the finish line is never too far away. The euphoria and satisfaction you experience afterwards is your reward. You can go home, have a beer and lie down for a bit without feelings of guilt. You have earned it.

It is different for longer endurance events, which can be anything from four hours to days or even weeks. The physical pain takes on a more chronic nature and thereby a different meaning. There are additional threats in the form of energy depletion, dehydration, overheating, undercooling and injuries, and not to forget the boredom which comes with the monotony of engaging in one particular activity for hours on end. In adventure racing you can add navigation and sleep deprivation to that list. I experienced many of these challenges in 2001 when I took part in an event called the Mizone Endurazone Multisport Race, also going by the name the Wild Places Challenge. The race started in Bluff, the southernmost place on mainland New Zealand, and finished 2787 km north at Cape Rēinga. Every day, depending on the terrain, 64 of us biked (mountain or road), kayaked (sea or river) and/or ran (usually off-road) for 6–12 hours, ducking in and out of the wilderness. It gave me an intimate insight into how my fellow Kiwi competitors coped with adversity and discomfort. Where I only just tolerated the inevitable suffering associated with these types of events, my fellow (Kiwi) competitors seemed to ignore the hardship, and even welcomed and embraced it, true to the Kiwi spirit. When I asked them how they viewed and experienced the challenges they encountered, they shrugged their shoulders, not understanding the question. Suffering, I learned, has a significant mental component, as it relates to how we process and perceive the physical, mental, geographical and weather-related challenges encountered.

Somehow I did get to Cape Rēinga. The adversity I experienced surpassed anything I had expected. I never managed to ignore the suffering. Embracing it was out of the question. But, inspired by my fellow Kiwi competitors who seemed mostly oblivious to it, I was able to accept its presence for the duration of the event. Competing in that month-long race felt like a rite of passage, and by finishing, I had passed the test.

After the Wild Places Challenge, I vowed to never do similar events again. I stuck to my word – mostly. The exception was the Ironman World Championship held in Hawaii in which I competed in 2013. The suffering I exposed myself to in that event was more intense than what I had experienced during the Wild Places Challenge, but at least it was all over within a day. Other than that, I managed to avoid the temptation to enter longer-distance events and thereby the physical and mental challenges that come with it. I stuck to the more familiar and bearable pain of the shorter-distance triathlon races. Until 2018, the year I turned 65.

In the year prior I had read an article about the (inaugural) 2016 Tour Aotearoa, a 3000 km unsupported mountain-bike tour covering the length of New Zealand. The Tour started at Cape Rēinga and finished in Bluff, going in the opposite direction to the Wild Places Challenge in 2001. The Tour route followed existing mountain-bike trails, connected by back-country roads.

It appealed to me, as it was not a race – it was called a brevet, a long-distance, non-competitive endurance race. To get your brevet, all you had to do was finish in less than 30 days. A minimum of 100 km per day on the bike did not sound excessive to me. I calculated that it would take me a good half day to cover that distance, leaving plenty of time for rest, relaxation and sightseeing. What a way to see the country and celebrate my sixty-fifth year! Surely I could do this event at a leisurely pace and enjoy, rather than endure, it and in the process put some of my demons from the 2001 Wild Places Challenge to bed!

As the Tour was unsupported, I needed a reliable bike, had to be well organised and be able to navigate the course. Logistics, organisation and navigation have never been my strong points, so I decided to invite a friend, one who could compensate for my deficiencies and provide some company at the same time. John Hudson, Huddy to his mates, seemed the perfect fit. He is one of those friends I would happily go to war with; he's courageous, reliable, loyal, meticulous, and a great organiser and planner. Huddy discovered cycling at a later age and found that he was good at it, and he showed all the enthusiasm that comes with that discovery. When I presented the idea of taking part in the 2018 edition of the Tour Aotearoa to him, he accepted immediately.

Neither of us were mountain bikers. We were roadies. The weeks of preparation included training sessions with fully laden mountain bikes. We soon worked out that the Tour Aotearoa would not be as easy as we had initially thought and that our planned daily distance ration of 110–120 km was going to take considerably longer than half a day. But we were committed and neither of us wanted to be the first to question our decision.

Huddy and I planned to travel and experience the country in a leisurely and enjoyable way. As often happens in life, fate had other plans. Huddy and I encountered more adversity than you can shake a stick at. Huddy had to quit the Tour on Day 3 through circumstances beyond his control. From then on, I was left to my own devices. Challenging terrain, injuries, illness, rain and more rain accompanied me on my journey south. I had to rely on all my experience and apply all I had learned over the years from the Kiwi sporting psyche to keep going. My daily contemplations while on the move helped me pass the time and distract me from my troubles.

When redlining it during a short-distance race, your attention goes to everything that has to do with getting to the finish line as fast as you can. You concentrate on your breathing, rhythm and technique. You anticipate the terrain ahead and you try to keep an eye on your competition. There is no time for contemplation, for thoughts, other than 'keeping it together'. You resist the little voice inside your head which says 'enough!' Instead it is 'push, push, push'.

Not so when training or racing over longer distances. To conserve energy, you go at a submaximal pace, which gives you the opportunity to let your thoughts run free. Over the years, during longer training sessions, I have solved many problems, from domestic and professional issues to world affairs. While swimming, biking and running, I have thought up innovative ways of training and racing for the athletes I coached and I have written many articles and books.

Multiday events, like the Tour Aotearoa, are also done at a controlled pace for the same reason: preservation. There is plenty of time for problem solving and contemplation during the long days, riding slowly through all types of weather conditions and landscapes. But there is only so much conscious deliberating you can do before your mind takes on a life of its own. Random thoughts bubble to the surface without you having much control over it. When this happens it is both worrying and liberating at the same time. It is a welcome distraction from the discomfort and fatigue, and it helps pass the time. The mind-numbing monotony of turning the bike pedals over and over again, day after day after day, should not be underestimated. Even the at-times spectacular scenery is not enough of a distraction, and the only thing left is to let your mind wander and explore its nooks and crannies.

In the evenings, I hammered my ruminations from the day onto my laptop, regardless of how tired I was. It became a cleansing ritual that helped me make sense of my daily experiences and embarrassments. I called it my administration. This publication is the end result. Enjoy!

John Hellemans

INTRODUCTION

The first and most important item we require for the Tour is a bike. Huddy goes straight to the shop and buys a nice new, shiny mountain bike painted battleship grey and as light as a feather. The bike is called Scott.

I have a look inside my shed and dust off an old bike which requires so many repairs and new parts that, by the time it is ready, I have spent as much money as Huddy has on his brand-new bike. After all that, I am told by a good friend, who is an experienced bike touring guide, that my bike will not be strong enough for the trip through the wilderness. I have run out of money and borrow a proper mountain bike from another friend, who lives in Golden Bay and has a garage full of bikes. The bike is called Spot and the frame is built from old-fashioned steel. Spot bikes are considered boutique bikes. I do not care, as long as it gets me from one end of the country to the other. For a boutique bike this one looks a bit haggard. I have to fork out more money for repairs and new parts.

* * *

Huddy and I plan to test our bikes and ourselves with an overnight trip from Christchurch to Akaroa and back to see if we are up to the task. The distance is 90 km one way. This does not sound much, but the back

Some hills on Banks Peninsula are so steep we have to walk.

roads we travel on are mainly gravel, it is hot and there are lots of big hills. Some are so steep that we have to walk. It is hard work.

I recognise it and get to work but, for Huddy, the experience is an eye-opener, or rather, an eye-closer, as by the time we arrive in Akaroa he collapses on the couch in our motel unit. He does not look well. I secretly hope that after this experience he will propose that we give up on the idea of biking the length of New Zealand.

But by the next morning Huddy has tarted himself up to the extent that he looks half decent again, and while I am still getting dressed he calls out, 'C'mon, what are you waiting for? We need to get going.'

A fellow endurance athlete near Christchurch . . .

And off we go – on a different route from the previous day, but it is still hot and there are still plenty of hills.

Close to home, I spot some donkeys in a paddock beside the road. I have always liked donkeys and we stop to say hello. It is obvious that Huddy finds all this a bit weird, but he is used to odd behaviour from me and takes it in his stride. I explain my admiration for donkeys which is based on their ability to cover long distances carrying heavy loads. 'We will be like donkeys when we do the Tour,' I quip. 'Speak for yourself,' Huddy laughs before he leads the final stretch into Christchurch while I contemplate what it would be like to be a donkey. Well, I will find out, won't I!

We have several meetings to plan the logistics, what to take, work out the route, and how and where to spend the nights. It is a frantic time for both of us, but more so for Huddy, as for him details are important.

He thinks about everything that could happen during our upcoming trip, including so many disasters that even I, who has seen it all (well, almost . . .), get worried.

Huddy insists we take a tent for emergencies. I am not keen to carry any unnecessary load and protest. Huddy insists. I suggest another practice trip to Akaroa and back, this time taking the tent. That way Huddy can experience what it means to not only carry an additional load but also to have to pitch a tent at the end of a long day and share a very small space for sleeping with a donkey.

When we squeeze into our little tent after a long day, Huddy is so tired from the day's work that he is asleep even before his head hits the pillow. But I have a restless night. I am kept awake by so many different noises coming from inside and outside the tent that even two sleeping pills do not knock me out.

As Huddy has slept like a baby, he still maintains that we bring the

I will be the fool who will have to carry the tent.

tent on the Tour. I agree reluctantly, knowing full well that I will be the fool who will have to carry it.

The day of departure is coming closer, and with that Huddy's excitement is growing by the day. I envy his optimism. My mood is more sombre, as I have an uneasy feeling about what is awaiting us.

* * *

The evening before our departure to Cape Rēinga, the starting point of our adventure, we have our final planning meeting at my place. Ien, my better half, has made a beautiful meal for us. 'The last supper,' I think sombrely. I have learned through experience that whenever I am away for more than two days I miss home terribly. I have come to accept that it is just how I am.

Huddy is in good mettle, busy announcing further additions to the list of things which can go wrong on our journey. This gets me into an even gloomier mood. I had noticed that every time we had a meeting Huddy arrived in a state of agitation and turmoil, but somehow by the end of the meeting he had cheered up considerably, having shared all his concerns about our upcoming adventure. This was in contrast to me. I always turned up at the meetings in a relaxed state and with a calm mind, which is my preferred state of being. Invariably, by the end of the meeting it was my head which buzzed with tension and trepidation as if Huddy's state on arrival had been contagious.

Huddy announces proudly that he has already packed his bike and other gear. This is despite the fact that we are not flying north till the afternoon of the next day. He warns me that he had difficulty fitting his bike into the bike box. I mull his words over and realise how much I still have to do. Panic sets in. Oblivious to my state of mind, Huddy engages with Ien and tells entertaining stories. Suddenly, I stand up and say to Huddy, 'You'd better go now.' Huddy gets the hint and scuttles off home.

The next hour, in fading light and attacked by a thousand mosquitoes, I work frantically to get my bike into the cardboard box I had obtained from a bike shop. In the end, the bike slips into the box rather easily. I am not sure what Huddy had been on about and decide to bring my earplugs on the expedition – and not just to help me sleep.

* * *

The next day we meet at Christchurch Airport with plenty of time to spare, as we want to make sure that our bikes fit on the plane. When we arrive in Auckland, we are too mean to take a shuttle or taxi to our hotel, so we walk and walk . . . and walk, as the hotel is much further than we thought. We also discover the reason why I got my bike into

We walked and walked, from Auckland Airport to our hotel.

the box so much easier. Spot's box is almost twice the size as the one for Scott.

The bus to Cape Rēinga.

* * *

The next morning, we wake up to a beautiful day, well suited for biking except for the fact that first we have to get from Auckland to Cape Rēinga by bus, a distance of 420 km, which will take the best part of the day.

We bike to the assembly point, which is not far from the hotel. Here we meet other Tour riders, who are ready to get on the bus. To call the bus we travel in 'battered' is an understatement. First registered in 1985, it has done enough miles to have circumnavigated the world at least twice. The bus seats are worn and so close together that my knees are jammed hard against the seat in front of me. The back of the seat is straight, at a 90-degree angle to the seat, and not flexible at all. Neither is the bus's suspension, which is rusted solid. It makes for a most uncomfortable ride as my back has seen better days and is easily upset.

Huddy, in contrast, is as happy as a sandboy. His legs are shorter than mine and his back is still in pristine condition. The upshot of all this is that Huddy's knees are finding plenty of space, and his back is coping well with the uncompromising seat and non-existent suspension. Huddy talks and sings and makes lots of new friends during the trip, oblivious to my misery. He even falls asleep for a while, much to my disgust.

All the bikes, and there must be at least 50, are tied on a large trailer which is towed behind the bus.

The bus stops in Kaitāia. It is already past five o'clock and we decide to have dinner rather than heat up a freeze-dried meal in our cabin at Waitiki Landing, not far from the Cape, where we are spending the night. The only restaurant open in Kaitāia is McDonald's. We don't mind, as we don't often get a chance to indulge in fast foods; our wives make sure of that. We know full well that the uplifting effect McDonald's has on our mood will not last long and does not weigh up against the long-term detrimental effects on our physical health. The end result, as always, is a slight sense of disappointment and guilt, but at least it is a feed.

That night, we go to bed early. While Huddy is soon fast asleep, I am mulling things over and bemoan the fact that this whole journey is already a lot more complicated than I envisaged, and we have not even started cycling. Surely the biking can't be as hard as the bus ride, or can it?

<u>DAY 1</u>

A DAY AT THE BEACH
Cape Rēinga to Ahipara – 103 km

We get up at the crack of dawn and board the dreaded bus one more time to cover the final 20 km to Cape Rēinga. Cape Rēinga is a sacred place where, according to Māori tradition, the spirits of the dead leave Aotearoa. It is here that they leap off the headland into the water to travel to the afterlife. They surface briefly at the Three Kings Islands, singing a last lament for loved ones, before departing for their spiritual home in Hawaiki. When I contemplate death I like the idea that my spirit will go to a place where there is an abundance of milk and honey, and where I will meet up with old friends who have gone before me. But I don't believe any of it. I am overawed by the beauty of the Cape's dramatic landscape, with its steep cliffs and huge sand dunes. It is also here that the Pacific Ocean and the Tasman Sea merge.

Day 1: Cape Rēinga – official send-off and blessing.

The colour changes from dark blue to azure, and the ripples and waves indicate the place were the two seas meet. We have our photo taken at the lighthouse before an official send-off and blessing by Ihirangi Heke, a respected Māori elder, who is doing the Tour also. It adds to the spirituality of the occasion.

Just before the start, while everyone in the group, consisting of about 60 riders, makes their last-minute preparations, a rumour swirls around that the first rider has arrived in Bluff in 10 and a half days.[1] I am impressed, as this means that he covered an average of 300 km per day. I tell Heke the news. He responds with, 'Why the hurry?' That makes me think. He is right; why the hurry?

I like the Māori people and their culture. Their philosophy of not hurrying, the importance of whānau, and their idea of sharing and guarding the land, rather than owning it, is in stark contrast to the impatience, individualism, greed and competition of my own Pākehā culture.

Huddy and I are planning to get to Bluff in 27 days. This will give us three contingency days.

The starting gun goes off at 9 am. We are happy to finally be on our way. As a bonus, we are served up fantastic weather in the form of a stark blue sky and a solid tailwind. The Cape Rēinga lighthouse is situated high above the sea, so it is mainly downhill to get to Ninety Mile Beach.

I carry a heavy load. The advantage of that is I am fast on the downhills without having to do any work for it. I pass a lot of riders that way but am wise enough not to celebrate, as I know that there

---

1 For logistical reasons, the 525 participants of the Tour Aotearoa start in six groups of 60–80 riders over a period of 18 days through the month of February, with the first wave departing on 10 February. We are in the second-to-last wave, leaving Cape Rēinga on 28 February.

Day 1: Te Paki Stream.

Day 1: Spot and Scott get intimate on Ninety Mile Beach.

is a price to pay and, indeed, on the few uphill sections I am left well behind. Soon the field spreads into small groups and single riders.

After an hour, Huddy and I reach Ninety Mile Beach, but not before having to ride down the shallow Te Paki Stream, which runs towards the sea in between the dunes. We get our feet wet, which we don't like, but our bikes are worse off; they get soaked and have sand all through their chains, bottom brackets and derailleurs. We give them a quick shower with clean river water when we reach the beach and have a short rest while they dry out in the afternoon sun. Ninety Mile Beach, or Te Oneroa-a-Tōhē, is the longest beach in New Zealand. Truth be told, it is actually only 55 miles (88 km) long. The early settlers guessed the distance to be 90 miles, as their horses could normally cover 30 miles per day. They did not count on the slower pace when horses travel on soft sand, but the name stuck.

With help from the tailwind we make good progress for the first few hours. We enjoy ourselves and exchange stories. But gradually the wind

Day 1: That's where we're going . . .

turns and the tailwind is replaced by a headwind. By then, we have been on our bikes for six hours and we have had enough of the sand, the sea, and the sun burning on our backs, necks and legs. We slog it out for another couple of hours in silence, arriving at our destination in the late afternoon, eight hours after our departure. Huddy's GPS shows an average speed of 15 km/hr. I am disappointed and decide that it must have been the soft sand which slowed us down. Little do I know that 15 km/hr is a solid pace for a fully laden mountain bike and that there will be many sections where my average speed will be well below that.

DAY 2

TĀNE MAHUTA
Ahipara to Waipoua Forest – 120 km

Day 2 turns out to be a big day, and not only because of the distance. The hills are unrelenting, one after another. The total climbing we do is more than 2000 metres, according to Huddy's bike computer. In my younger days, I was one of the best in climbing hills, on foot or on the bike. But that ability has eroded exponentially with age. Huddy is less experienced but shows a lot of perseverance and keeps up all day, not complaining once, like a true Kiwi. I did not think the Tour was going to be that tough and develop a newfound admiration for him.

It is 64 km from Ahipara to Rāwene and there is only one watering hole, which is at Broadwood, the halfway point. When we stop there for refreshments, we find that other riders before us have plundered the shop, leaving only leftovers.

One of the highlights of the day is a 10-minute ferry ride across the Hokianga Harbour, which looks magnificent under the clear blue sky, its turquoise-blue surface as smooth as glass, broken only by the bow of the ferry. After a leisurely lunch in Rāwene, we continue via the picturesque coastal townships of Opononi and Ōmāpere to the Waipoua Forest, home of Tāne Mahuta, the largest kauri tree in New Zealand, estimated to be between 1250 and 2500 years old. It stands proudly in the middle of the forest, towering over the younger trees like a king. 'Imagine if Tāne could talk,' I say to Huddy while I look up at the giant tree. 'He would have so many stories to tell about the early days of New Zealand. We would finally find out the truth.'

Huddy looks at me incredulously, grins and says, 'Don't worry

Day 2: Endless Northland hills.

Day 2: Tāne Mahuta, Lord of the Forest.

Day 2: The Hokianga Harbour.

Day 2: Watering hole at Broadwood.

mate, even if he could talk, he won't. If he tells the truth about what happened in the past, nobody will believe him and he will be chopped down to be silenced.' I look up at the mighty tree which looks to be nodding, in agreement with Huddy's words.

We leave Ahipara at 7 am and arrive at the Waipoua Forest Campground nearly 12 hours later, where we share a small cabin with bunk beds. Huddy is in bed by 8.30 pm. I stay up a bit longer to do my administration. Today, once again, we have been lucky with the weather. I wonder how long that will last.

DAY 3

HEADWIND AND RAIN ANNOUNCE THEIR ARRIVAL
Waipoua Forest to Parakai – 120 km

When I wake up the next morning and look out of the window of the cabin, the weather looks still favourable. The forecast for later that day is not so good so I want to get on the way. Huddy is still rolled up in his sleeping bag and I give him a push. He moans softly.

'What's wrong?' I ask.

'I had a terrible sleep. I woke up in the middle of the night with my heart going haywire and I don't feel at all well,' Huddy replies.

I tell him to harden up and this time I give him such a hard shove that he falls out of bed, which has the desired effect.

The day's ride starts with a big hill climb. Huddy starts to feel better once we reach the top. This is good, as once again the hilly terrain is

Day 3: Ready to battle the elements.

challenging. Just as well that the weather is still favourable to make the hard work bearable.

At lunchtime we reach Dargaville, where Huddy consumes a large sausage and me two tasty custard squares. We need to get to the Kaipara Harbour to take a ferry across to Parakai. Just when we decide to get back on our bikes, the news filters through that the ferry has broken down. Instead of a ferry, a bus will bring us to the other side of the harbour. The bus will pick us up at Maungaturoto, 70 km south-east of Dargaville.

The weather changes as soon as we remount our bikes. Headwind and rain make their first appearance.

I wonder if, in the spirit of the Tour, we should bike the 90-km stretch between Maungaturoto and Parakai, rather than take the bus. But I do not say this out loud, as a bus ride sounds more appealing than doing a whole lot more biking with a headwind and rain for company.

Day 3: Out of luck at the Matakohe café.   *Day 3: The driver of the bus to Parakai is a dead ringer for Father Christmas.*

Progress on the gravel roads is slow. We are looking forward to finding some shelter in the only café between Dargaville and Maungaturoto, located in Matakohe, but we find it closed. As if that is not enough, soon after, my front carrier collapses onto my front wheel. The carrier is just too heavily loaded. I make some running repairs and we hurry on.

The bus will leave Maungaturoto at 5 pm, and by now we are well behind schedule. Missing the bus will finish our horror day off nicely.

When we arrive, drenched and tired, just after 5 pm, we see no bus or any other riders, and with our heads down we decide to retreat into a café to confer what to do next. There we discover that a little luck is still with us as we are welcomed by a whole bunch of other soaked, rowdy bike packers still waiting for the bus to arrive. We should have known, as timetables in Northland are as accurate as a pig counting to 10.

An hour later the bus arrives. A man who looks suspiciously like Father Christmas is the driver. Perhaps it *is* Father Christmas, I contemplate. On the way we discover why the bus is the preferred way to travel along this stretch of highway: the road has no shoulder to speak of. We nearly run over a couple of Tour riders who decided to bike the extra distance rather than take the bus. The driver does not even look back to see if they are okay, which makes me decide that he definitely can't be Father Christmas.

It is dark by the time the bus drops us off at a motel in Parakai. We have a soak in the hot pools that the town is known for and settle in for the night.

DAY 4

THEN THERE WAS ONLY ONE
Parakai to Hūnua – 120-plus km

Today is a sad day. Huddy was once again poorly overnight with a haywire heart – so poorly that I have to bundle him into a taxi very early in the morning to send him to a hospital in nearby Auckland to be checked out. I take the opportunity to dispose of the tent by quickly shoving it into the taxi without Huddy noticing. 'Good riddance,' I think, referring to the tent.

Suddenly I am alone. Panic sets in. Now I have to do all the logistical and practical thinking myself. Huddy has done most of that till now, which left me free to contemplate and daydream to my heart's content. Today, especially, I need Huddy more than ever to navigate through Auckland, the biggest city of New Zealand. Navigation has never been my strength. I need arrows, signs, cones and marshals to point me in the right direction. Huddy has given me his Garmin cycling computer, which has maps and GPS, but when I press the 'On' button, it starts to speak to me in Italian. I quickly turn it off again.

Today I am going to get lost, that is for sure. I decide to leave early – so early that it is still pitch-dark. That is the first of many mistakes I will make today. Except for pitch-darkness, it is also raining heavily and the road is very busy with angry trucks and impatient early-morning commuters. I am tooted at, nearly run over and sprayed soaking wet by trucks which roll through the large puddles on the road without any consideration for a lone cyclist.

I feel lost, even if I am not really lost, as the map lighting up on my mobile phone indicates that I am still on the right road. I contemplate the fact that feeling lost and being lost are two different things. Without Huddy I *feel* lost, and know that it is unavoidable that I will *get* lost sooner or later. I smile a wry smile at such clever thinking, but my mind quickly turns to more practical matters, like staying alive when a large truck comes thundering past, so close that I am nearly sucked under its large wheels.

The rain is replaced by a headwind, and I go down on my aerobars to reduce frontal resistance and relieve the pressure on my backside. Coming into Auckland, I see a long queue of the same cars that had whizzed past me before. I can't help waving at them but only get grumpy looks in return. 'Who wants to live in Auckland?' I think.

I am passed by a lot of commuters on e-bikes. First it makes me angry; there I am, slogging it out with my heavy load while these cheats fly past me, hardly pedalling and with only a small bag hanging off their shoulder. Thinking about it a bit more, I wonder what it would be like to ride an electric bicycle. Perhaps I should try one out; it certainly looks fun. I have always considered electric bikes as fake bikes. But now I decide that we live in fake times anyway, with all the fake news, so what's wrong with joining the fakers. But to use one for this tour would be cheating; it will have to wait. I file the thought away in my brain under 'wishful thinking'.

With the Garmin out of action, I use a map on my mobile phone together with the written instructions in the Tour guide for navigation. Both are strapped onto my handlebars. With one eye on the map and guidebook, and the other on the road, the inevitable result is several wrong turns, near crashes, and a massive headache. At one stage, I cross the same bridge for the third time. Soon after that, the battery of my mobile goes flat and I have to rely solely on the directions in the little guidebook.

At Mount Eden, I climb to the summit, as that is a photo check-point.[2] When I come back down the hill a bit later at a great rate of knots I miss the turn-off I should have taken. I realise this too late and I decide to take a short cut to get back to the actual route. This gets me well and truly lost. Just when I sit down on the side of the road wondering what to do next, a staunch-looking mountain biker with bendy legs comes past. I recognise him as a Tour rider by his heavily laden bike and absent stare. He looks as if he knows where he is going. I jump up, mount my bike and chase after him.

When I catch up with him he ignores me. I don't mind, as long as he knows the way out of Auckland. We cruise along at a good pace when I hear a phone ring. The sound comes from the other rider's backpack. We stop and he gestures that it is his wife, and that it might take a while so I should carry on. This leaves me alone once again. At least by this stage we are on the outskirts of Auckland.

Then I make my umpteenth mistake for the day. When I am freewheeling down a steep hill I enjoy the exhilaration of the speed but, in the process, I miss the turn-off halfway down the descent. I see

---

2 Participants of the Tour have to take photos of specific landmarks during their journey as proof that they have done the prescribed route.

Day 4: Maungawhau/Mount Eden.

Day 4: An escapee with a black eye.

the sharp left turn as I fly past it and I know that that is where I have to go, but I am making such good speed that I carry on regardless. Once I arrive at the bottom of the hill and come to my senses, I have to turn around and bike back up again.

It is getting towards the end of a long day, but at least I have left Auckland behind me. The roads are hilly but much quieter and with fewer turns to choose from.

I come past a white bunny with one black eye sitting on the berm at the side of the road. I think 'am I hallucinating?' and stop to take a photo as proof that what I see is real. On closer inspection it looks to be a domestic rabbit which must have escaped. It does indeed have one black eye, but not from trauma. He must have been born with it. As daylight is fading I have no time to rescue him from passing cars or angry dogs. I wish him well and say goodbye.

Tired and hungry, I arrive just on dark at the Bike Bunker Lodge near Hūnua. There are many other Tour riders staying the night, but I am too tired to make conversation and I go to bed early. But not before calling Huddy to see how he is. He explains that his haywire heart got such a fright when the doctors announced they would have to stop and restart it that it spontaneously reverted to his normal healthy rhythm. That is the good news. The bad news is that the doctors advised him not to continue the Tour. It goes quiet on the other end of the line and for a moment both of us consider the consequences. I vow to continue the Tour, also on his behalf, for as long as I can.

DAY 5

MORE TROUBLE
Hūnua to Matamata – 164 km

On Day 5 I am in a hurry, as I want to see my whānau, who are waiting for me in Matamata, my destination for the day. Not only will Ien be there but also my youngest daughter Saar, her husband Mark and, most importantly, my two granddaughters, Ocean (nine) and Lakey (six).

I leave early as there is more than 160 km to cover, the furthest I will have gone on any day of the Tour so far. To get to Pūkorokoro-Miranda (famous for its shorebirds), I chose the inland route option over the more scenic but busy coastal road. A headwind makes life difficult for the first 80 km, which also includes the bike trails along the windswept shores of the Firth of Thames. Mid-morning, I feel myself weaken. I am overcome by a wave of fatigue which is more than the tiredness that comes with hard work. To make matters worse, one of my legs goes lame. 'The wheels are falling off,' I think bleakly. But when I look at Spot's wheels they are not really fallen off, as they are still going round in circles, albeit very slowly. The only thing threatening to fall off (my bike) is me, that is how slow I am going. I decide to stop thinking, to save energy and concentrate on staying upright.

Te Aroha consists of a few houses and a couple of shops. Nobody ever gets lost in Te Aroha. Except today – I do. It's a world first. I blame my empty state of mind, so I rekindle my thinking. My muscles do not respond any more to my commands. But in my semi-conscious state, every now and then a picture of my whānau waiting for me on the side of the road in Matamata flashes before my half-closed eyes, and that spurs me on.

Somewhere on the endless flat and quiet back roads between Te

Day 5: Grandkids, the best medicine.

Aroha and Cambridge a lone car passes by and stops on the side of the road. The doors open and out step Huddy and his wife Helene. They got concerned that it was taking me so long and have come looking for me. They hydrate and feed me, lift me back on Spot and give me a push in the direction of Cambridge. They know me well enough not to suggest that I hitch a ride with them.

Just when darkness hits, I crawl into Matamata. My whānau is nowhere to be seen. They got sick of waiting and went to the pub, where I find them. My two granddaughters don't recognise me. It does not help that I have grown a beard. I left my shaving kit at home to save weight and make room for my laptop. Ocean looks me up and down and asks, 'Opa, is that you? You look like you are ninety years old!'[3]

Huddy, whose good health has returned, is there as well, accompanied by Helene.

Huddy notices that I am not up to much that evening and assists me with my preparations for the next day. I feel lousy and I doubt I will be able to continue, but that decision can wait till the morning when I wake up. Or rather, if I wake up.

---

3 Opa is the word for 'granddad' in the Netherlands, where I was born and raised before I settled in New Zealand.

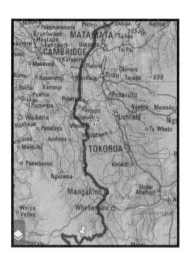

DAY 6

TAILWIND COMES TO THE RESCUE
Matamata to Mangakino – 90 km

Feeling sorry for yourself is never helpful. It does not assist the process of problem solving, and it certainly does not make you feel any better. The next morning I am grateful for waking up. I stretch my body and move my limbs ever so gingerly. They are still working, so that is a good start.

Huddy joins me for the first part of the day's journey towards the Waikato River Trail. I am happy about this and everything feels as it should. Huddy leads the way. At the start of the trail, we are joined by our wives. It is a jolly time for all.

But I still do not feel right. I suffer from a sharp pain on the back of my head, as if I have been stung by a thousand bees. But bees are nowhere to be seen.

We have lunch at the Rhubarb Café in Arapuni. Somewhat embarrassed, I ask Huddy to have a look at the beestings on the back of my head. Huddy, who happens to have a medical degree, has one look at my scalp, and says, 'Mate, that looks like shingles.' I know about shingles. It is a virus which creeps into a nerve and causes pain and a skin rash. It can affect any part of the body; in my case it is the back of my head. I protest and ask Huddy if this is not an affliction more common in older people. 'Exactly,' he replies with a wry smile. Huddy, Helene and Ien rush back to Matamata to get some drugs from the pharmacy for my shingles. Ien will meet me again in Mangakino that evening, so I can start on the pills. That is if I do not perish on the way. The diagnosis does explain why I felt so dreadful yesterday, as the virus was already well awake and multiplying in my body.

Day 6: On the Waikato River Trail.

After I have said goodbye to the others, I slowly work my way south along the bike trails and back-country roads which run through the dairy farmland of the Waikato. There are cows everywhere. It feels as if they look at me in disdain. Some moo at me when I bike past. I give them the one-finger salute. It is a safe thing to do, as I am shielded from them by a barbed-wire fence.

My lame leg is still not working well and, combined with a bruised bum from sitting on the bicycle seat for hours on end and the stinging on the back of my head, it all gets a bit much. What saves me is a gentle tailwind which is at my back for most of the day. Headwind finally gets his chance towards the end of the day, but by then I am saved by a long downhill stretch into Mangakino.

On arrival I take a handful of the pills Ien has brought with her and another lot a while later for good measure. I hope that there are sleeping pills among them. I need a good night's sleep.

I am grateful to Ien, Huddy and Helene for being there for me when it matters. It makes me more determined to push on. Quitting is not an option – not yet.

DAY 7

THE TIMBER TRAIL
Mangakino to the Timber Trail Lodge – 95 km

I feel better the next morning, but just to make sure I take another handful of pills before departing. I feel surprisingly cheerful. Perhaps Huddy put some happy pills into the mix.

I go through the morning ritual of attaching one bag onto the rear carrier and another underneath my aerobars, a system which seems to be working well. I check the tyres, make sure all the gears are working and put a bit of oil on the chain. Spot has performed magnificently until now and I realise I need to look after him to keep it that way.

I follow a narrow track which runs along the shores of Lake Maraetai. A low mist hangs over the lake while the sun is trying to break through. It gives me a sense of peace. I remind myself that the early morning is often the best time of the day. Perhaps this tour is not so bad after all –

at least I experience a lot of early mornings.

A little later, while my thoughts are still running free, I suddenly realise that the written course instructions tell me something different from what the map on my phone shows. Lost again. I swear under my breath. I have decided a long time ago that swearing out loud is never helpful. It does not make you feel good and others get easily offended or upset and it can spoil the whole atmosphere. When you swear in silence others are not affected by it. I do this only when things go against me, which happens, as we have learned, not infrequently. I tell myself off and turn around to find the correct turn-off.

The sun comes out in full and a tailwind once again comes to the party. I make good progress and do not get lost again.

The written instructions tell me to veer off the road and cross over a swing bridge. The swing bridge looks narrow and not very safe. It is

Day 7: Leaving Mangakino.

Day 7: The centre of the North Island.

Day 7: The well-signposted Timber Trail is 84 km, with 35 bridges.

also a long way down to the river below. I don't like heights. The bridge is very narrow and as soon as I push my bike ahead of me the pedals poke through the wire netting of the bridge on either side, stopping Spot dead in its tracks. I try to untangle the pedals, which makes the bridge sway dangerously. Slowly and gently, I push Spot across the bridge, all the while untangling the pedals. It is a slow, laborious job.

I make up a song. 'We are not afraid, as we don't want to be late (for dinner)', and sing the song to the melody of 'God Save the Queen'. It helps me to get across the bridge.

For the next 40 km I cross serious mountain-bike country with rough tracks, rocks and lots of steep hills. I have to concentrate hard not to crash. The track brings me to the point which is called the Centre of the North Island. Here I have a morning tea break.

The Timber Trail starts not long after this landmark. Other

mountain bikers have told me how wonderful the Timber Trail is. I agree, but the best thing is that it is well signposted. It must be one of the best signposted bike trails in the world. Even in places where there are no turn-offs in sight and there is nowhere else to go than to follow the trail, there are Timber Trail signs, reassuring me that I am still on the right route. I can finally relax and enjoy the ride without the fear of getting lost. The newly built Timber Trail Lodge, located halfway along the trail, provides me with a meal and a bed for the night. It has been a good day.

WORRIES, SINGLE TRACK TRAILS, GRAVEL ROADS AND A SPRINKLE OF ASPHALT
Timber Trail Lodge to Ōwhango – 95 km

I wake up the next morning with lots of worries swirling through my head. I don't know why; it is just a feeling of unease. The back of my head is on fire from the shingles and I am not hungry. I force myself to eat some breakfast. I am joined by a couple of hard-out bike packers, the first of Wave 6, which left two days after my 5th Wave. I have met Elke and Keith before on a more formal occasion. Elke is the daughter of well-known New Zealand mountaineer the late Gottlieb Braun-Elwert. Under his guidance she climbed Aoraki Mount Cook, New Zealand's highest mountain (3724 m), at the age of 14. She explains that she is doing the

Day 8: Early morning leaving Timber Trail Lodge.

Tour to get some light relief in between her mountaineering exploits. Keith is the inventor of the Robo-Kiwi bike packing bags. I am impressed with their progress. I study their bikes and see that they have all their gear perfectly balanced in small bags strapped to the handlebars, in between the frame and behind the saddle. Before I have a chance to take a photo of their nifty bike set-ups, they are gone.

It is another beautiful morning, with mist hanging in and around the trees. 'Why the worry?' I think. I took a handful of pills earlier and am waiting for the effect to kick in. I know that being worried is unhelpful. Why should you worry about something which hasn't happened? And if something does happen, it is generally not as bad as what you expect it to be, and if it is as bad as what you think it might be, well, then somehow you will cope and find a way to carry on. I read this somewhere and I try to live by it, but I don't always manage to do so. Like today.

The track is rocky and bouncy one moment and boggy the next. I need to concentrate to stay upright. An hour into the ride I feel hot and stop to take my jacket off. I put it in my backpack. While I stand on the side of the track, I notice the stillness, interrupted only by the chatter of the birds. My mood improves and somehow I feel lighter when I continue.

I enjoy the feeling until I realise that the reason for the lightness is not my improved mood but the fact that I left my backpack behind. It contains my vital belongings like money, credit card, maps, phone and, most importantly, my laptop containing my administration. This whole journey will be in jeopardy if I do not find my backpack. I retrace my route with twice the speed, as now I am really worried. What if I can't find the spot where I had stopped? Everything looks the same in a native forest. What if someone has taken it? But I know that it is unlikely, as there is no one else around. This is called 'catastrophic thinking': a trap which is easy to fall into when in a panic. I get more and more convinced that I will never see my backpack again.

Just when I decide that I have gone well past the point where I had stopped, I see the red backpack lying on the side of the track. Relieved, I strap it extra tight onto my back to continue my journey at a more sedate pace.

There are plenty of swing bridges, which freak me out, but I sing my way across. The trail continues to be a bumpy ride, up and down, through ruts and muddy bogs. Especially the latter are of concern. The bogs are driest on the outer edges and so it makes sense to go either to the far left or to the far right. Except that I keep having difficulty deciding which side to choose, left or right, and as a result steer Spot mostly straight through the middle, the bog's boggiest point. Several times I get stuck and I even fall over a couple of times. Every time, I am determined to do better at the next bog, but my indecisiveness gets the

Day 8: Owhango Lodge, a welcome sight at the end of a long day.

better of me and through the middle I go. I once again realise that at heart I am a roadie. I long for a bit of asphalt where I can get down on my aerobars and stomp on the pedals while my thoughts run free, not having to concentrate on staying upright.

Finally, at the end of the morning, after a long stretch of gravel road, there is some asphalt. By then the temperature is close to 30 degrees and I am getting hungry and thirsty. I stop at a place called Taumarunui. I have never heard of Taumarunui, but there is a café and that is all that matters.

Only 26 km to go. 'Not far,' I think, but I have not counted on the fact that most of it is uphill and on gravel roads, so the kilometres tick by ever so slowly.

At around 6 pm I arrive in a state of exhaustion at my destination of Ōwhango. The Owhango Lodge has seen better days; a shabby exterior and stepping inside is like going back to the 60s and 70s. The cook, who is also the receptionist and bartender, notices my depleted state and serves me half a chicken, accompanied by a pile of chips and a corn cob, with ice cream and cake for dessert.

The only other guests in the hotel are an elderly couple travelling on motorbikes. They are wearing matching black T-shirts with a dazzling silver logo of a motorbike on the front. The man can hardly walk. He shuffles and his legs seem to give way with every step.

I put two and two together and ask him if he has been involved in a motorbike accident.

'No, mate,' the man answers, 'I just walked the Tongariro Crossing.'

I have walked the 20-kilometre-long mountain crossing once, in my younger days. In fact, I ran it. I remember it as a spectacular route and quite tough, but not so tough that I had been unable to walk afterwards like this geezer.

The man explains that he had not been able to do any training, as his joints are shot from years of playing rugby. He adds that his partner, who still walks with the energy and bounce of a foal, has never played much sport, not even netball, but she walks every day for miles with her girlfriends. It had been her suggestion for her husband to do the walk. It would do him good.

Funny how women know what's good for their men. It seems to happen with most married couples. I have not been immune from this phenomenon myself.

The couple go to bed early, straight after dinner, while I sit down in the lounge of the hotel to do my administration. I have come to the realisation that I am the only Tour rider who carries a laptop. But I am reluctant to part with it, even if it means carrying less weight.

I am just finishing up, ready to go to bed, when there is a knock on the window. In the dusk I can see the vague outline of two haggard faces. One of them is gesturing and mouthing if there is still accommodation available. On closer observation they have bikes with them. They must be Tour riders.

I let them in and explain that the cook, receptionist and bartender have all gone home. The two look pretty shattered and I feel sorry for them. Reluctantly I offer them the spare beds in my bedroom. My fear that a good night's sleep is jeopardised by my generous offer is confirmed as soon as the light goes out and a snoring recital of impressive proportions starts up.

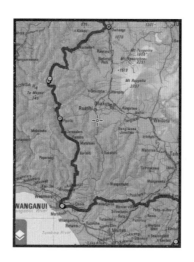

A HISTORICAL DISCOVERY
Ōwhango to Whanganui – 160 km

The snorers get up early, devour their breakfast and leave. It is still pitch-dark. They take little interest in me, moping about after my fitful sleep. Through the window I can see the lights from their bikes disappear into the distance. It is too late to get back to sleep and too early to leave. After my early-morning experience on Day 4 I try to avoid riding in the dark. I have a leisurely breakfast and I pore over the information outlining the route for the day.

There are two options. First there is the formidable Kaiwhakauka tramping and mountain-bike trail, known for its mud, tree roots and treacherous cliffs. The trail ends at Mangapūrua Landing on the banks of the Whanganui River where jet boats pick the riders up at appointed times for the last 30-km stretch to Pipiriki. This worries me. What if I am late and miss my designated jet boat? On top of that there is a storm brewing, and not just any storm – it is the remnants of a cyclone, and weather warnings for heavy rain are out all over the country. I have visions of carrying my bike on my shoulder in a downpour on a narrow, muddy and slippery track between a steep rock face and a vertical drop. One slip and I will disappear over the edge, never to be found again. 'Tour rider vanished in Kaiwhakauka wilderness, presumed dead' the headlines in the papers will read.

The alternative to the mud and uncertainty of the Kaiwhakauka Track is what is commonly called the 'chicken route'. This substitute route is a fair bit longer but it is on asphalt roads. It follows State Highway 4 through the national park for 55 km before turning off at Raetihi onto the Pipiriki–Raetihi road to Pipiriki, the point where the jet boats drop the riders off who choose to do the Kaiwhakauka trail. I do not have to think long – the chicken route it will be. After the Timber Trail I have had enough of rocks, tree roots, mud and falling over.

Day 9: The peaks of the Volcanic Plateau seen from State Highway 4.

I start at first light under a clear sky, with little wind and temperatures in the mid-teens – excellent biking conditions. The tops of Mount Ruapehu and Ngāuruhoe are peeking out above the layered clouds which hang just below their summits. I get down on my aerobars and admire the asphalt flashing by underneath.

I wonder how the 'chicken route' got its name. I first heard the expression when I learned to kayak. 'To take the chicken route, you take the inside of the bend in a fast-flowing river. It is flatter, safer and less scary than staying in the middle where the water flows faster and is much wilder', we were told by our instructor. He had his gaze fixed firmly onto me, or at least that is what I imagined, when he finished his sermon with 'the chicken route is for the less brave'. During the kayaking course, I became a fan of the chicken route. Why choose a more treacherous route over a safer option, even if it takes a bit longer (that is, if you don't capsize in the rough stuff, which happened to me the one time I got overconfident)?

I consider it unfair on chickens to call the easier route after them. What do they know? Very little, as chickens have very small brains. They don't know anything about easy or difficult routes, they only scatter, and that is not thinking, that is doing without thinking. They can't even cross a road, despite the frequently asked question 'Why does the chicken cross the road?' And the standard answer, 'To get to the other side', is nonsense. A chicken only crosses the road if it has a death wish. But even that is impossible, as their brains are too small to contain death wishes or to understand the meaning thereof.

I am rudely awakened from my contemplations when I am side-swiped by a large truck. I end up in the loose gravel beside the road and decide to take more notice of the traffic coming from behind. I wonder what would be worse: getting lost in the jungle of the Kaiwhakauka Track or ending up splattered on the highway as road kill, like the chicken who crossed the road. Is a quick death on the road to be preferred over a slow one in the jungle?

From Pipiriki the country road beside the Whanganui River is still sealed, but not very well, and there are many roadworks along the way. But I am used to that from Christchurch after the 2011 earthquake. I notice that my health and confidence are returning. The stinging on the back of my head is replaced by a more tolerable dull ache. The pills must be working.

The predicted tropical storm is nowhere to be seen, and I continue happily through the spectacular landscape of the river valley. When I approach a small settlement, to my astonishment, the sign on the side of the road announces 'Jerusalem'. I stop. Do I see that right? Jerusalem? I always believed that Jerusalem was located in Israel/ Palestine, but no, it is right here, smack bang in the middle of New Zealand. All of a sudden I feel a bit religious, despite the fact that I am not the religious type. I find it too difficult to come to grips with the

Day 9: Signpost for Jerusalem (Hiruhārama).

different religions, all claiming their God to be the only true God. I believe in nature, as there is only one nature and it is undeniable, right there, in front of our eyes, in all its splendour.

Despite all this, I am excited to discover that there is a Jerusalem located in New Zealand, even it if looks a bit different from what I had imagined. It suddenly occurs to me that there is a Bethlehem in New Zealand as well. Originally it was a small, independent town, but more recently it has been swallowed up by its bigger cousin, Tauranga, and has become one of its suburbs. In deep thought about my discovery I continue on.

The next settlement I pass is called London. 'No way,' I exclaim aloud, but the place-name sign does not lie. When the next little village is announced as Athens, I am hardly surprised any more. Can it be that once upon a time New Zealand was the cultural and religious centre of the world, and not Europe or the Middle East? History is rewritten all the time, so why not in this particular case? Napoleon Bonaparte,

Day 9: London (Rānana) and Athens (Ātene) on the Whanganui River.

the French statesman and military leader during the time of the French Revolution, said, 'History is a set of lies agreed upon.' I couldn't agree more, with the evidence staring me in the face not once, not twice, but thrice, right here in the middle of the North Island of New Zealand. The Bible has also been rewritten many times since its inception, and over time the translators could well have become confused about the exact locations of Jerusalem and Bethlehem. I get a headache from contemplating the possible consequences of my discoveries. For example, where will this leave the Māori, as the indigenous people of Aotearoa?

I contemplate what will happen when we tell the world that civilisation started down under, in little old New Zealand. It is likely to be considered fake news and generate a lot of comment from representatives of different dominations, or is it denominations? I learn later, however, that there is a more prosaic reason for the existence of these names. Māori asked the missionary Richard Taylor, operating in the area in the 1840s, to provide some biblical names for their settlements along the lower Whanganui River. Other non-biblical names such as Rānana (London), Ātene (Athens) and Koroniti (Corinth) were thrown in for good measure.

I decide to take a break from these complex thoughts and focus on getting to my destination for the day. I roll into Whanganui in the early evening, but not before I am soaked to the skin by the first shower of the promised rain.

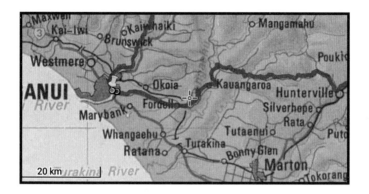

DAY 10

WET, WETTER, WETTEST
Whanganui to Hunterville – 60 km

When I wake up the next morning it is raining cats and dogs. Of course, it does not rain cats and dogs for real, as it would be dangerous to go outside. Umbrellas would not do the trick. 'Hosing down' is therefore perhaps a better metaphor, or 'bucketing down', although I wonder who turns the hoses on and who fills and empties the buckets, and what would happen if whoever fills the buckets lets go of a bucket by accident, or deliberately, and the bucket lands on someone's head. Who would be responsible? And can you insure against being hit by a flying bucket? These thoughts go through my mind when I stare intently from behind the window at the rain, wishing it to go away.

I take the opportunity to catch up on my administration. I am resigned to the fact that I will never be totally on top of this task, as that is not in my nature; it is always a work in progress. My laptop, which is my desk, represents a wilderness of randomly placed icons, apps and documents, resistant to any systematic order. I admire people with a clean and orderly desktop.

At 10 am the rain has still not abated, so I choose to risk it. At least I can finally trial my full rain kit. Within minutes, I am soaked to the bone. My 20-year-old kayaking jacket does not cut it. The only part of my body which stays dry is my head, courtesy of a mighty-big plastic contraption fitted around my helmet. A dry head is important for thinking and contemplation.

I cross the bridge over the Whanganui River. The instructions say to enter a tunnel in Durie Hill at the other end of the bridge. At the back of the tunnel, I find a lift with a bell beside it. I ring the bell and with a lot of banging and shaking a lift comes down. When the doors open, it feels like I am back in time. The décor of the lift's interior fits right into the early 1900s, with its worn-out blue carpet and timber-covered

Day 10: A dry head is important for thinking and contemplation.

Day 10: Whanganui's Durie Hill War Memorial Tower.

sides. The lift is serviced by a grumpy elderly lady who looks as tired as the lift. She gives Spot a foul look and checks the tyres before she lets the bike in. Fortunately, the rain has washed them squeaky clean. I pay the lady two dollars and try to make conversation. I ask how old the lift is. 'Ninety-nine years old' is the short answer, and then we are at the top of the hill.

When I step out of the lift, the first thing I see is the Durie Hill War Memorial Tower, which is so high that the top disappears into the rain clouds. The tower is a monument in honour of the fallen soldiers from the First World War. I always feel sad when I see these war memorials which are sprinkled throughout the country. They have rows of names of fallen soldiers who hail from the region written on their columns; young men who fought for a king or queen from the other side of the world. Go figure. But I know that their effort contributed to the liberation of Western Europe, including the country in which I grew

Day 10: The former post office, Hunterville.

up, in the Second World War, and for that I am forever grateful.

The tower can be climbed, but it is still raining heavily. That, combined with my fear of heights and the fact that I am already well behind schedule, makes me decide against it.

I make slow progress, lashed by the rain and wind which seem to come from all directions. I am passed by another Tour rider. She is tiny, of dark complexion and she has a smile on her face. The weather does not seem to bother her.

'Hello,' I say. 'I am John.'

'Hello, John,' she replies. 'I am Amy.'

But Amy is on a mission and has no time for small talk. She accelerates up the road, her spindly little legs dancing on the pedals, a perfect picture of grace and harmony despite the conditions.

Then it is just me, Spot, heavy rain, headwind, hills and a couple of slips on the road where I have to wait while a group of orange-vested labourers clear them up.

Ten kilometres before Hunterville, I am passed by two brothers, Ray and Alan, who are doing the Tour together. I slot in behind them and enjoy the protection from the wind.

We arrive in Hunterville at 3 pm. I am not even halfway to my planned destination for the day. But I have had enough of the rain and book into the Station Hotel where a whole lot of other Tour riders turn up as well. Together we watch a one-day cricket match between New Zealand and England. The match is decided in New Zealand's favour with the last ball. I am not a great fan of cricket, but I join in the cheering, not wanting to be a spoilsport.

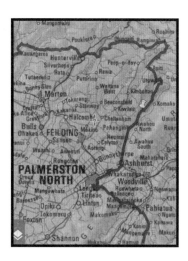

DAY 11

DIGGING DEEP

Hunterville to Palmerston North – 140 km

The next morning it is still raining. This time I don't wait, because that strategy had not worked the previous day and, more importantly, I want to try to get to Wellington by Saturday.

My plan is to get to Palmerston North today, Masterton on Friday and Wellington on Saturday, a total of 385 km. Under normal circumstances, 385 km over three days is doable. But as my luck would have it, circumstances are far from normal. Rain and (head)wind are still dominating the weather pattern. Headwind has even called in his big brother Storm to give him a hand.

I decide to face the elements. Determined, I attack the mud-covered, wheel-sucking gravel roads. The rivers I cross are raging, slips block my way and there are more hills than you can shake a stick at. I ponder the fact that shaking a stick at one hill is easy, especially if the hill is close by, but trying to shake a stick at a whole lot of hills sounds rather tiring. I certainly will run out of puff if I have to shake sticks at the hills as well as climb them.

I plan to have a coffee in Rangiwāhia and lunch at the Apiti Tavern, but everything is closed. All the streets are deserted; there is no one around. I seek shelter in a draughty public toilet in Apiti where I eat some dry bread with a bit of cheese which I find among my emergency supplies. 'This must be the lowest point of my journey, surely it can't get worse,' I mutter to myself, munching on the bread, shivering from the cold and wet.

I continue on the open backroads of the Manawatū, unprotected from the driving rain, getting colder and more miserable by the minute. With 30 km still to go, I am passed by a ute with a gruff-looking farmer behind the wheel. The ute slows down and the farmer opens the window

Day 11: The Pohangina River (above) in flood and the Manawatū on a rainy day.

on the side where I am riding. He asks me if I want a lift. I panic. I am tempted but know that it will be cheating – unless I return to the exact same spot tomorrow to bike the hitchhiked section. But retracing my route the next day would mean not getting to Wellington on Saturday. How would I get back to the exact spot anyway? On my bike? That thought sends my brain into a spin.

The farmer senses my hesitation, and says, 'What's up, man?'

I shake my head, and cry out, 'I can't.'

'Suit yourself,' the farmer replies, and puts his foot down on the accelerator, disappearing in a cloud of mist.

I feel an immediate pang of regret. What have I done? But it is too late.

Ashhurst is my intermediate target; from there the distance to Palmerston North is a 'mere' 21 km. The guidebook promises that there will be a dairy in Ashhurst. I will myself on and arrive, chilled and soaked to the bone, and, yes, there is a dairy, owned by an Indian family, like most dairies in New Zealand. Today an older woman (grandma?), a middle-aged male (father?) and three kids of varying

Day 11: More rain clouds looming over the Manawatū.

ages are busy stacking shelves. They eye me up suspiciously when I enter their shop and the lot of them flee quickly behind the safety of the counter.

Who is this dripping, shivering man with a wrapped-up helmet still on his head (my hands are so cold that I have been unable to undo the helmet buckle)? I ask if they sell hot drinks, which they don't, but they do sell milkshakes. I have a cold milkshake which I drink in silence in front of the curious gaze of the five family members, who refuse to leave the protection of the counter. The drink makes me shiver even more. I hop back onto Spot and start to pedal furiously in an attempt to warm up.

I arrive in Palmerston North at dusk. I check in at a motel and hop straight into bed with the heater and electric blanket turned on high.

When my temperature has risen to more acceptable levels, I go next door to get a burger and chips. Surely I have earned it. I have an apple for dessert in honour of my dietitian wife. She does not like it when I eat colourless meals.

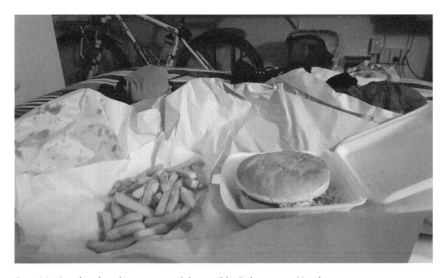

Day 11: A colourless but energy-rich meal in Palmerston North.

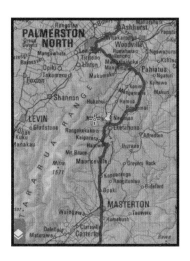

HOW MUCH MISERY CAN ONE TAKE?
Palmerston North to Masterton – 104 km

What one can do to oneself beggars belief. I contemplate this while I am climbing a massive hill just outside Palmerston North. The road winding up the hill, named the Pahiatua Aokautere Road, is known as a popular training hill for local roadies. That is all nice and well for a cyclist on a bike weighing a mere 7 kg, but it is a different story for a bike packer on a fully laden mountain-bike weighing at least 30 kg, plus of course my own weight, even if I must have lost a few kilos since the start of the Tour.

I am in a dark mood; not only because of the hill. First, I woke up late, which ruined my plan for an early start. In addition, I once again found adverse weather conditions waiting for me outside, with black clouds threatening in the distance and a strong wind coming from the south.

Of course I took a wrong turn trying to find my way out of Palmerston North, losing more precious time. I had always wondered why Palmerston North isn't the capital city of New Zealand, it being so centrally located, but now I know why: no one should be able to get lost in a capital city and it has also become obvious that the weather is not agreeable. This would put any politician in a grumpy mood, with bad policy making as a result.

I once coached an athlete who grew up in Palmy (as they call it deceptively, as it rhymes with balmy, which it certainly is not). This athlete always raved about his hometown, but now I know the truth.

As I crawl up the Pahiatua Aokautere Road, my mood gets darker still as I am attacked by one truck after another. There is little or no shoulder on the road, which is okay for the road, as roads have little use for shoulders, but not okay for non-motorised traffic like me on my bike. The trucks refuse to give me a wide berth, as they are supposed to. A couple of times my outside elbow brushes against the side of a truck, causing me to veer into the rough.

A couple of months before the Tour, I had read a letter to the editor in *The Press* in Christchurch from an irate truck driver who compared cyclists to maggots. I have nothing against maggots, but most cyclists' brains are much bigger than those of maggots (there are always exceptions of course) and to compare cyclists to maggots is at least derogatory. I can only conclude that the truck drivers on the Pahiatua Aokautere Road must concur with their Christchurch colleague the way they treat me, and many of the other riders, as I learn later. With drivers like that I despair that there is little hope for cyclists, let alone for world peace.

Day 12: Pahiatua Aokautere Road – no room for cyclists.

On the other side of the hill, I turn off the

main road onto a gravel road. This gets me away from the trucks, but not from my sombre thoughts or from the headwind. I have had enough when I come to Pahīatua. I stop for a break. It is lunchtime so I order an all-day breakfast which consists of eggs, bacon, hash browns, sausages, bread and a baked tomato. I wash it all down with a large flat white, let out a quiet burp and feel better for it.

Outside it is spitting, and I delay my departure by checking my phone, something I seldom do during work hours. There is a message from my good friend and at times mentor, Renzie Hanham.

Renzie: How are you feeling this morning?

Me: Not great. Not sure why I am doing this.

Renzie: I guess it will come down to the meaning and significance this has for you, not that you need me to tell you that, but I enjoy stating the obvious!

Me: Is it about never giving up?

Renzie: It's what underpins that and what gives that meaning. Never giving up is a useful attribute . . . often.

Me: Well, I'd better get on with it. Over and out!

Renzie: Indeed.

I get back onto Spot and tackle the gravel roads and headwinds with more vigour. For a while I make good progress. Another shot of caffeine in Eketāhuna, and I am ready to take on the final 35 km into Masterton.

The intermittent drizzle is replaced by persistent rain while the strong headwind is not abating. It is as if the wind and rain challenge each other to see who can do the most damage. It gets so bad that at one stage I plead with both to give me a break. The wind responds with a gust which nearly blows me off the road and the rain answers with a tantalising rainbow in the far distance, but without retreating.

With only 5 km to go, the heavens open. All available hoses are turned on; cats and dogs as well as bucket loads are all directed at me, a lone cyclist, moving slowly through the desolate grey and wet landscape of the Manawatū. A drowned rat must be a cheerful sight compared to me. I have never minded the company of a bit of misery, as I have learned that it tends to spur me on. Misery can be a motivator, but there is a limit. I feel that I am getting close to my misery threshold. I wonder how much more of it I can take.

Ien had offered to come to Masterton to meet me. I had declined her offer as I feared that seeing her would make me quit there and then. I always go a bit mellow and soft when I see her. But I am so desperately miserable that I hope she is going to be there waiting for me, regardless, with her happy smile (and a nice hot meal).

In the early evening, exhausted and soaking wet, I roll into the Mawley Holiday Park, where I have booked a cabin. Ien is not there, but I try to stay upbeat. I will see her tomorrow as I am still on schedule to get to Wellington.

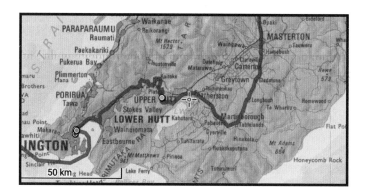

A SPECTACULAR FALL
Masterton to Wellington – 140 km

I am up before the crack of dawn and set off while it is still dark. It is cold. True to form I lose my way trying to get out of Masterton. By the time I find the road which leads me out of town, daylight is filtering through. There is no wind and the road is sealed, straight and almost flat. I work hard to keep warm and make good progress. Another rider comes past, says a quick hello, and accelerates. Hang on, I could do with a lift, and I sprint up to the other rider and settle in behind. He is unaware, as when he looks back 20 minutes later he reacts surprised.

'Have you sped up or have I slowed down?' he demands to know.

'Mate,' I reply, 'its called drafting.'

We start chatting, and I find out that his name is Wayne and that he is a psychotherapist from Nelson. That cheers me up no end. Have I finally found someone in whom I can confide my woes, someone who will not only understand but might also have some answers? But Wayne will have none of it. He interrupts me and asks what the highlights of my trip have been thus far. I can't think of any. I shake my head and ask, 'What about you?'

Wayne smiles. 'The Waipoua Forest was wonderful and so were the sand dunes before Ōmāpere and I loved the Timber Trail. There were just too many highlights.'

'Mmmm,' I think, 'this must be the difference between a pessimist and an optimist; between seeing a glass half empty or half full.' And I vow to do better and enjoy myself a bit more, like Wayne.

After 50 km we stop in Martinborough for a coffee and some food. Wayne is in a hurry, as he wants to catch the 4 pm Wellington to Picton ferry which brings the riders across Cook Strait to the South Island.

I order a second coffee and join another rider who is sitting at a

Day 13: The Remutaka Trail has some challenging sections.

Day 13: Paul (right) leads us through dark tunnels on the Remutaka Trail.

different table. Paul is from Wellington where he works in security. More importantly, he knows the route into Wellington. I ask if I can join him. Together we ride to the start of the Remutaka Trail, 70 km north of Wellington. Here we meet up with Ien and Ruthie, a good friend from Wellington.

The four of us ride the Remutaka Trail together and we have a jolly good time, even if it is hard work. We have to traverse through some long tunnels which are darker than the night. My headlight is not suitable at all, emitting a weak, spluttering beam. Paul comes to the rescue. As he is in security, he has a light so strong that no criminal, smuggler or tunnel can escape it. He leads the way, making reassuring noises directed at anyone who is a bit scared.

When we reach the car park at the end of the trail, Paul and I say a quick goodbye to the ladies. I will see them again in Wellington where Ien and I will stay the night at Ruthie's home.

Paul smells his home and pushes the pace. We follow the Hutt River Trail and I am surprised how beautiful the surroundings are. I always thought of Lower Hutt as an industrial area with state housing sprinkled in between the factories, but today I fancy myself in Switzerland while I am riding next to this sparkling, meandering river flanked by steep hills, covered in a thousand different colours of green. It helps that the sun has finally come out after all those wet, windy and grey days.

The technical difficulty of the Hutt River Trail is rated Grade 1, the easiest grade. Despite this, I manage to make a spectacular fall at a tricky switchback. I discover too late that there is a steep incline directly behind a sharp bend. Spot is in the wrong gear, stalls and bucks. With the front wheel in the air, I lose control and tumble backwards, bike and all, down a steep bank. I land hard on my backside with Spot on top of me. I lie still and do a quick body check.

Paul has heard a loud thud behind him and quickly turns around. 'Are you okay?' he shouts down the bank.

I quickly get up and assess the damage: a decent graze on one elbow and a sore butt.

When Paul realises that I am not seriously hurt, he bursts out laughing. 'Trust a Dutchman to crash on a Grade 1 trail,' he grins.

We arrive in Wellington in the late afternoon and part ways. Paul goes home for the night while I get spoiled by Ruthie and Ien with a beautiful meal of lamb and veges. For some reason, every time I eat lamb, I have to block out any thoughts of little lambs running, jumping and playing freely in the green pastures, unaware that their lives are going to be brutally cut short for the benefit of anyone who likes the taste of them. It is no different on this occasion.

After dinner, I watch the rugby on television. My second-favourite team, the Crusaders (my favourite team is the Highlanders. Go the Highlanders!), loses to the Wellington Hurricanes, but I do not let it spoil what otherwise has been a good day.

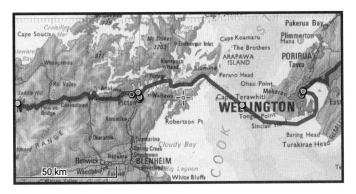

DAY 14

HUDDY MAKES A COMEBACK OF SORTS
Wellington to Nelson – 3.5 hours on the ferry and 110 km on Spot

I get dropped off at the ferry terminal early the next morning and line up at a sign which says 'Assembly area for bicycles, canoes, dogs'. The sun is out and there is no wind: perfect conditions for a smooth and scenic crossing. The highlight of the trip is a pod of dolphins which accompanies the ferry in the middle of Cook Strait.

Chomping on an early lunch, I am seated next to a Tour rider from Dunedin. He is a young-looking 49-year-old. We exchange stories and when we arrive in Picton we team up for the first part of the ride. We are happy to finally be on the South Island.

The Dunediner is a good bike rider and I can only just hold his wheel.

'You do any bike racing?' I yell out.

He shakes his head.

I tell him to get a road bike and join the Otago Cycling Club to do some events. He seems to like the idea and speeds up even more. He has the smooth, efficient pedalling stroke of a professional cyclist. I cannot help noticing talent when I see it. Even if this chap is a bit older, I know that he will have the better of some of the more experienced cyclists in his age group.

We left Picton after midday, so there is need for some urgency if we want to be in Nelson before dark. We stop for a quick lunch in Havelock and part ways a bit later at the Pelorus Bridge. The Dunediner will take the Grade 5 Maungatapu Track mountain-biking trail to Nelson. I have decided to take the chicken route, which follows the main highway. The distance is a fair bit more, but I still prefer the risk of road kill over bush kill.

Day 14: The Marlborough Sounds en route to Picton.

Day 14: The Pelorus River en route to Nelson. Inset – reunited with Huddy.

Day 14: Sunset over Tasman Bay.

A blue sky and a light tailwind keep me company on this 55-km stretch of road. Big climbs and long descents alternate with each other.

I am nearing Nelson when suddenly I see Huddy come sailing over the crest of a hill to meet me. Of course, he is not really sailing, as there is no water in sight and Scott does not look much like a boat.

It is a happy reunion. Huddy has brought Boycy along, a mutual friend. The three of us ride together for the last few kilometres into Nelson.

Boycy lives with his gorgeous wife Maree in a beautiful house at the top of a bastard of a hill on the outskirts of Nelson. Maree has offered to pick us up from the bottom of the hill with her truck, but none of us, being males and not wanting to be outdone, wants to be the first to call her, so we climb the bastard of a hill and curse in silence.

On arrival we have a meal together, accompanied by champagne. We propose a toast to friendship and to the South Island.

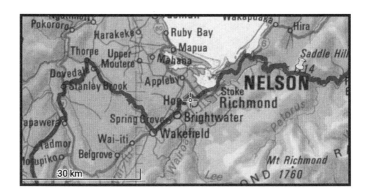

N/A

DAY 15

QUINTESSENTIAL NEW ZEALAND
Nelson to Tapawera – 80 km

I have the best sleep ever and wake up refreshed. I quickly do some administration, have breakfast and set out, accompanied by Boycy. He will keep me company till Dovedale, 40 km south of Nelson.

But first we stop off at Village Cycles in Richmond. Spot has started making alarming noises. I can't work out which precise part of Spot is creaking. I looked and listened but am none the wiser, so it is time to find an expert. The mechanic assigned to Spot looks like an exotic bird from South America as he carries an impressive bunch of feathers on his head in the form of a multi-coloured mohawk. 'He must be good,' I think. While the Mohawk is tinkering with Spot, Boycy and I find a café for a coffee and second round of breakfast.

When I return to Village Cycles I find Spot almost unrecognisable, with a glittering new chain, brake pads and rear tyre. I even catch a faint waft of eau de cologne coming from the derailleur, which is the signature of any good bicycle mechanic. I dream of having a treatment of some sort as well so I can look and smell the same as Spot, but I dismiss the idea as quickly as it comes into my head. What am I thinking?

For the first few miles riding Spot feels effortless and Boycy and I have a good many chats. The weather is perfect and the country roads scenic; there are rolling hills covered in native bush, interspersed with dry, grassy fields with sheep grazing. 'Quintessential New Zealand,' I marvel at Boycy, not quite knowing the exact meaning of the word 'quintessential', but it rolls off my tongue as if I do.

Together we ride up Dovedale Hill. I stop at the top. I want to take a photo of the view but can't find my phone anywhere. I look here, there and everywhere; I open all my bags and my pockets and some more,

Day 15: Tapawera in Tasman.

but can't find the blasted thing. Boycy tries to call my phone with his, but there is no ringtone. He tries again before he discovers that we are out of range. I conclude that I must have left it at the café or bike shop.

I decide to forget about it and come back to the issue at a later time, as I can only handle so many worries at any one time and I am already concerned about trying to find the way once Boycy leaves me to return to Nelson. Boycy reassures me that he will go past the café and bike shop on his way home to check.

We continue on, and just before we reach Dovedale, I hear a phone beeping in my backpack. Can you believe it? I can't, but stop anyway and empty my backpack onto the road, and there it is, in my breakfast bowl, hidden under a roll of toilet paper. I do not know whether to laugh or cry, so I do neither, but Boycy has a good laugh.

We say goodbye and I carry on alone through the valleys and over the hills of the province named Tasman after Abel Tasman. Abel Tasman is one of my heroes, but that is a story for another time.

I arrive in Tapawera in the mid-afternoon. Huddy and Helene are there already. They have been out on their bikes looking for me. Somehow they missed me, but now we are reunited. It is easy to find one another in Tapawera, as it is not a big place; actually, it is so small that I am convinced that I will find my way out of Tapawera the next morning without getting lost. Perhaps Tapawera should become the capital of New Zealand, or even the world. Everyone would get along as it is so easy to find each other and even easier to get out of the place when you want to.

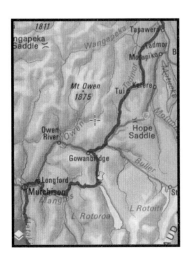

<u>DAY 16</u>

THE SANDFLIES ATTACK
Tapawera to Murchison – 96 km

The distance for Day 16 of just under 100 km is deceptive. I have learned the hard way that the course profile, riding surface and wind direction need to be calculated into the estimated time it takes to get to my daily destination. Gravel roads halve my speed compared to asphalt, and single tracks halve that again, and uphill, well, most of the time uphill biking is done at a walking pace.

Today has 60 km of gravel with a lot of climbing. I meet ferocious headwinds as soon as I leave Tapawera and turn into the Tadmor Valley. I fight hard not to be pushed back to where I came from and crawl up the gradual incline to the Tadmor Saddle, 500 metres above sea level. Ominous-looking clouds pour over the top.

As if on cue, as soon as I arrive at the highest point, the heavens open

Day 16: A tranquil Lake Rotoroa.

and the rain joins forces with the wind to challenge me once again. But I am better prepared this time. I put my rain jacket and gloves on and decide to 'embrace my environment' in true Kiwi spirit. I will welcome whatever comes my way today. I have tried this technique at times in the past, with varying degrees of success.

Today I succeed in embracing the environment. Despite the concerted efforts of wind and rain my spirits remain high. Lake Rotoroa is my intermediate goal. I arrive at midday and stop at a backpackers lodge that has a sign advertising coffee and muffins. The place is run by an old man who is short of breath and unsteady on his feet. He makes me a pot of plunger coffee served with a muffin as big as a medium-sized SUV. He seems a bit lonely, so I stay for a bit and hear him out.

By the time I get back on my bike, the rain has disappeared and the clouds have lifted, exposing Lake Rotoroa in its full glory. I stop to

Day 16: The lake was peaceful, but the sandflies weren't.

take some photos but am immediately attacked by the only dangerous animal inhabiting New Zealand: the notorious sandfly. They live mainly on the West Coast, with Lake Rotoroa as their headquarters. They attack me in their thousands, and I have no chance against the vicious creatures. I try to swat them away while putting copious insect repellent on any exposed skin, but to no avail. In desperation, for a short moment, I consider drinking the stuff, but think the better of it. I admit defeat and jump on my bike. 'Out of here,' I cry out loud.

The climb up from the lake to the Braeburn Saddle is steep and rocky. I have to keep my wits about me, as the loose rocks on the gravel road threaten my balance as I slowly grind uphill. What does not help is that I am itchy from the sandfly bites. It turns into a torturous ascent. The breeze which meets me on the downhill on the other side cools my skin, and I slowly get my mojo back. During the descent I steer Spot rather recklessly through a number of overflowing fords which cross the gravel road.

Huddy and Helene meet me on their bikes and accompany me for the final stretch into Murchison, where we bunk down in a motel for the night.

PRINCESS JACINDA
AND HER FISHERMAN
Murchison to Reefton – 122 km

I want to get on the road early, as there are a couple of passes to cross on the way to Reefton. The Maruia Saddle and the Rahu Saddle are each 600 metres above sea level. I have packed plenty of food, as for the first 80 km I will be in the wilderness, well away from civilisation.

I set off in the dark and meet up with another rider from Auckland, a builder by profession. I have always been in awe of builders. I am good at breaking stuff and taking things apart, but it stops there. I have never built or repaired anything successfully. The builder is of Dutch descent; we get on well and talk about this and that. But he is too strong and I have to let him go.

This gives me time to contemplate. The soft light which comes

Day 17: Among the beech forest of the Maruia Saddle.

with the early dawn reveals low-hanging clouds, thick native bush and mountain streams with crystal-clear water, conducive for contemplation.

Princess Jacinda pops up in my head. I am worried about her. She is the new prime minister but also carries a little prince or princess in her tummy. I wonder how Princess Jacinda is going to combine motherhood with her busy job managing the affairs of her country. I admire Princess Jacinda. It is clear that she has a brain which is quick-firing and multi-dimensional, able to address different issues at once. She can be firm, empathetic, compassionate, diplomatic and decisive, all at the same time. This is rare for a politician and for example in stark contrast with the cocky rooster who is currently President of the United Sates. He must have a small brain, limited and one-dimensional in its functioning.

Princess Jacinda is engaged to be married to a man who has the

Day 17: The soft light of the early morning reveals low-hanging clouds and thick native bush.

name and looks of a film star, which, in a way, he is. Clarke Gayford can be seen on national television, catching big fish, which has made him into a legend, as anyone who can catch a really big fish is called a legend in New Zealand. I tend to disagree. First of all, I believe that you cannot be a legend until after you are dead. Also, I consider fishing cruel and not deserving of legendary status. Imagine being a fish, just swimming along minding your own business, daydreaming, nibbling at some seaweed or a crab, seeing a tasty-looking piece of dead squid floating by to eat, and suddenly, whammo, before you can scratch the back of your head, you have a hook the size of a crayfish leg through your

Day 17: Mountain streams with crystal-clear water.

lip, or your eye, or your ear. No, not your ear. It is called something else. What is it? Yes, a gill. Fish breathe through their gills. Next you are jerked up to the surface and into the air, which you don't like, as you cannot breathe air; you can only breathe in water, which is why you have gills and why fish can never drown. The worst thing is still to come, which is when the fisherman or woman tries to take the hook out of your face. It needs a firm hand and not all fishermen and women have that. After that, if you are lucky you will be thrown back in the water. You float on your back for a while to come to your senses and thank your lucky stars, despite the fact that your lip is bleeding or you are minus one eye, or half a jaw, before you quickly swim away.

I wonder if Clarke only throws the fish back when he is on television, just to look good. Perhaps, other times, he knocks the fish on the head to bring home for dinner. It is said that fish have no brains

Day 17: Close encounter with Jack Lovelock.

and therefore feel no pain. What nonsense. Look at the fish flounder, wrestle and gasp when they are caught. You can only do that when you have a brain. Same for thanking your lucky stars, which is what fish do when they are given a second chance. Thirdly, a fish has a memory, as, after he has been caught a few times, he is more careful and more difficult to catch. For memories you need a brain. So there is all the evidence you need for the existence of a fish brain. True, it is small; the size of a seed. If his brain was a bit bigger, a fish would surely notice a big hook dangling in front of its nose before taking a bite of whatever hangs off it.

Clarke has promised that he will take time out from fishing to look after the little prince or princess once it is born to allow Princess Jacinda to continue with her work of taking care of the nation. But it is not easy to look after a baby 24/7; fishing is much easier. He might regret it and want to go back to fishing. Time will tell, I conclude.

In the meantime I make good progress and arrive at Springs Junction at lunchtime. I treat myself to a large omelette with ham, cheese, tomato and no onions. With the omelette on board, I tackle the 8-km climb to Rahu Saddle. The final 36 km into Reefton is all downhill and on asphalt, so I am hoofing it.

I am met by Huddy, when I close in on Reefton. We come through Crushington, the birthplace of Jack Lovelock, who won the gold medal in the 1500 metres at the 1936 Berlin Olympics in a dramatic finish. In its heyday, Crushington was a vibrant settlement, famous for its quartz-mining. It was named after the pervasive sound of quartz being crushed by the mine's machinery. All that's left now is a little-known memorial on the side of the road dedicated to Lovelock. We stop to pay tribute to the great runner before we jump back on our bikes and race each other into Reefton.

FOOLING THE WEATHER GODS
Reefton to Kūmara – 120 km

Today the plan is for a quick 80 km from Reefton to Greymouth, all on asphalt. It is the 'chicken route' option. The off-road alternative, called the Big River Trail, which is 56 km long, is introduced in the course book as a '5- to 7-hour challenging stage, not passable if it has been raining, as there are several river crossings'. Heavy rain is predicted for later that afternoon. I am convinced that I will not get through the Big River Trail by late afternoon, or late evening – or ever, for that matter – so I have a valid excuse.

I enjoy the safety of the asphalt on the back roads of the West Coast. The by now familiar low cloud and drizzle adds to the mysterious landscape of lush native bush, gentle rolling hills and, at times, mountain tops breaking through the grey.

I make good progress and arrive in Blackball mid-morning. Blackball was once a flourishing mining town, famous for the daring strikes by miners for better pay and working conditions in the early 1900s. On the back of miners' strikes in Blackball in 1908, and a growing labour movement nationwide, Princess Jacinda's New Zealand Labour Party was formed in 1916. In 1925, Blackball became the official centre of New Zealand radicalism when the New Zealand Communist Party shifted its headquarters there from Wellington.

As I have leftish sympathies, I look forward to visiting this historic place. I plan to have morning tea at Formerly The Blackball Hilton. When it was originally called the Blackball Hilton, after the local mine manager, the hotel owners had a lawsuit on their doorstep from the big Hilton Hotel chain before the paint on their sign had dried. I think this is rather petty. The Hilton Hotel chain owners could have looked at it in good humour, considered it a compliment and donated the town one per cent of their profit as a thank you. Blackball would

Day 18: Looking back at Reefton.

Day 18: Formerly The Blackball Hilton.

have prospered. But that is not how directors of big profit-making companies work. They will not make big profits if they buy into my philosophy, which is for wealth to be shared by all, but they might well be much happier if they did.

Much to my disappointment, I find the Formerly The Blackball Hilton closed. I have a lukewarm instant coffee at the local shop instead.

And who shows up in Blackball on his bike? None other than Huddy. That cures my disappointment on the spot. Together we ride on to Greymouth.

Day 18: Photo check at the infamous Greymouth Bar.

We arrive at the Top 10 Holiday Park just after lunch. I am getting ready for some rest and relaxation when I realise that I have missed the photo control point at the Greymouth Bar where the Grey River meets the Tasman Sea.

Ien will arrive in Greymouth later that afternoon and I want to be clean and smelling like roses by the time she arrives. I quickly put my bike pants back on, hop onto Spot and race to the bar to take the compulsory photo.

Over the years, the tumultuous water at the mouth of the Grey River has claimed many ships; too many to shake a stick at. I contemplate that you have to be mighty quick to shake a stick at a sinking ship, as it will have disappeared under the surface before you have found a suitable stick.

On my return, Huddy and I discuss the plan for the next day. Heavy rain is in the forecast. Huddy suggests that I ride the first 30 km of the West Coast Wilderness Trail to Kūmara that afternoon. Once in Kūmara,

Day 18: The start of the West Coast Wilderness Trail between Greymouth and Kūmara.

Huddy will pick me up with his car to bring me back to Greymouth. The next morning, he will drop me back off in Kūmara. As a result, I will not have to ride so far in the predicted pouring rain the next day.

I find that a cunning plan. Huddy is well and truly making up for his departure from the Tour at Day 3, not that he had a lot of control over that. He turns up on his bike at unexpected times, often towards the end of the day, when I am at a low, to accompany me for those last few difficult kilometres, and he thinks and plans with and for me. I can't really wish for a better partner for the Tour. For the third time that day, I strap my bags onto Spot, put my bike pants on and set off to Kūmara with a tailwind for company. I am excited by the thought that I am in the process of fooling the weather gods. I have never managed to trick them before; usually it is the other way around.

On the way to Kūmara, I wonder if hitching a ride back to Greymouth with Huddy could be considered assistance. Tour Aotearoa is supposed to be a non-assisted event. But then, the car will take me in the opposite direction of the tour route, which can be considered anti-assistance, or even a hindrance. But that will be cancelled out by the drive back to Kūmara the next day, so I decide that it should all work out well in the end.

While I am on my secret mission, the promised weather front is closing in from the south and starts spitting at me from a distance. The clouds burst when I enter Kūmara, just in time.

When I get off my bike to shelter on the veranda of the local pub to wait for Huddy, I spot Ien driving past. She is coming from Christchurch and is on her way to Greymouth to meet us. The expression on her face when she spots me is priceless. Huddy turns up at the same time and the three of us have a drink in the pub to celebrate our reunion.

It has been a good day. Fooling the weather gods is the highlight. I know that they will not be happy, that they will want revenge, but I decide not to worry about that for now.

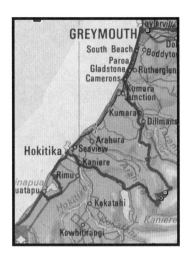

DAY 19

MINDFULNESS
Kūmara to Hokitika – 70 km

When I get up the next morning, the wind and rain are lashing at the windows and sliding doors of our motel unit, bursting with anger and energy. I imagine that the weather gods are furious to have been outwitted. 'Come out and play with us,' they jeer.

But I just stand there, calmly considering my next move. I decide to let the rain and wind rant and rave for a while. I am not in a hurry as I have already done 30 km of today's route. I can afford to start a bit later. I gather that sooner or later the ferocity of the weather must diminish.

That is exactly what happens. At 10 o'clock it is dry. Huddy and Ien drop me and Spot off in Kūmara at exactly the same spot where I finished my ride the previous day. From here I depart to tackle the remainder of the West Coast Wilderness Trail. I have done this trail before. I look forward to it, as it is a beautiful ride on well-groomed trails through native forest. A bonus is the fact that because I know the route it will be less likely that I will get lost.

I have decided today to stay in the moment and not let my mind wander too much. Yes, I am going to have a day of mindfulness. But soon I can't help myself, and let my mind wander off to the future, to later that day when I will meet Ien and Huddy again. I also allow my mind to go to the past, to my memories. I enjoy playing with my memories. I have learned to remember the good times and not think about the bad ones too often. I wonder if anticipation for the future and thinking about old times are allowed when practising mindfulness. Can living in the moment be combined with bringing up the past and planning for the future?

Parts of the West Coast Wilderness Trail have turned into a river due to that morning's rain storm, but I splash through the water

Day 19: West Coast wilderness.   *Rain turns parts of the trail into a river.*

unconcerned. I celebrate my rare victory over the weather, and Spot needs a good wash anyway. The sun is trying to peep through the breaking clouds.

At the halfway point of the West Coast Wilderness Trail is a place which goes by the unusual name of Cowboy Paradise. Cowboy Paradise has a shooting range, accommodation and a restaurant in the form of a saloon. A pub, yes, that I can understand. I have seen many on my travels – far too many to shake sticks at. I would have developed a sore shoulder from all the shaking. There are pubs sprinkled everywhere throughout the countryside, even in places where there are no houses at all. But a saloon with a shooting range, now that is weird. They only exist in the Wild West of America.

The view from the deck of the saloon is stunning, dominated by the Arahura River down in the valley, and flanked by native-forest-covered

Day 19: The view from Cowboy Paradise is stunning.

Day 19: Hokitika, a welcome stop on the West Coast Wilderness Trail.

mountains. I take a photo and have a hot chocolate and poached egg on toast before I remount Spot to continue my journey.

The trail meanders downhill to Hokitika. Halfway, I meet Ien and Huddy and together we ride to Hokitika, where we are welcomed by Warren and Karolien, old friends, who have travelled over from Christchurch to meet us.

When we arrived in New Zealand many years ago, Warren and Karolien, aided by other friends, welcomed us and introduced us to the intricacies of life in New Zealand. Most importantly, Warren explained the rules of rugby to me. These rules are so complicated that, even after living in New Zealand for nearly 40 years, I still get confused – but I do not let on. I suspect that most Kiwis are like me and just pretend they know the rules, except of course for Warren, who knows them better than anyone.

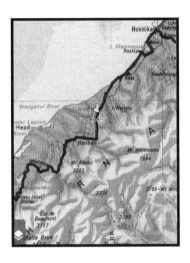

BODY CHECK
Hokitika to Franz Josef – 140 km

Day 20 is a big day. By now I know that 140 km on a fully laden mountain-bike with big, fat tyres (sorry Spot, but your tyres are fat) is very different from doing the same distance on a lightweight road bike with slim tyres which hardly touch the surface. I am accompanied for the first stretch to Ross by Ien, Warren and Karolien.

We depart early. When the sun appears from behind the distant hills, she winks at me – all good for today. There is no wind or rain in sight.

We arrive in Ross mid-morning. Time to stop for a coffee, but also for me to say goodbye to Ien and our friends.

I still have over 100 km to go. Once again I am by myself. I enjoy the sun, the scenery and a hint of a tailwind, which has sneaked up from behind. Life is good, even if I miss Huddy's company. Huddy is always

Day 20: The sun appears from behind the distant hills.

good for a story or two, which helps the time pass. Now I have to make up my own stories, which I have never been good at. I don't remember many and even when I do, I will get to the finish only to realise that I have forgotten how the story ends, so the whole thing becomes a bit of a fizzer. I am better at contemplation, but today I do not feel like it. Instead, I do a body check. I should have known that whenever one does a body check one always finds things wrong, and this time it is no different.

Here is a warning for the discerning reader. If you belong to the vast majority whose eyes glaze over and who tap their feet impatiently when someone volunteers their bodily ailments, then read no further. Skip the rest of this chapter and move on to the next. But if you have a keen interest in the suffering of others, or if you are a doctor (good learning), read on.

I start the body check with my feet, which often go numb, especially towards the end of the day, but at this stage they feel fine. Via my lower leg I go up to my knees, and an alarm bell starts ringing as I notice my left knee to be pretty damned sore. The pain has been coming on for a few days, but I have managed it so far by ignoring it. But now that I am paying attention to it, I can't ignore it any longer. I stop, take a pill and rub some ointment on the knee. I know full well that this is unlikely to do any good. I have never responded well to pills for any ailment I have suffered, except for sleeping pills – and the big pills Huddy gave me for my shingles, as they seem to have done the trick. The pills were the size and shape of a hand grenade. No wonder they were effective; if I were a virus, I would also go into hiding if one of these big mammas came my way. The only sign left of the shingles is a crusty, itchy scalp. I can just reach the spot with my fingers for a good scratch through a vent in the back of my helmet, but I have to be careful, as I nearly crashed a couple of times attempting this while riding along.

Next up is my backside. The more compassionate reader will have wondered how my bum is faring after 20 days on a bicycle seat. It is sore. There are two types of saddle pain: one is caused by sores you get from chafing, which causes the skin to peel, blister and fester. The second type is triggered by bruising of the tissue between the skin and the bum bone from the continual pressure and bouncing on the saddle. I suffer from the latter form of buttock pain. I started the Tour Aotearoa wearing one pair of cycling pants. After four days I added another to get some more cushioning. In Greymouth I added a third layer, but all to little avail.

The remainder of the body check, besides a mild ache in both shoulders and stiffness of the neck, is uneventful. In the end, I decide that only two ailments and some residual itchiness from a previous affliction are not bad for someone who has biked as far as I have.

I stop for lunch in Harihari, just over the halfway mark. I order a sausage and egg pie, a custard square and a fruit drink. That should get me through most of the afternoon.

With 30 km still to go I start to tire, just when a strengthening headwind makes an appearance to let me know that he has not forgotten me.

I stop in Whataroa and find the sandwiches Ien has made for me that morning. I feel a bit better after eating these and arrive in Franz Josef just before five o'clock.

As soon as I reach my unit at the local holiday park, I collapse on my bed, still in my biking gear, including shoes and helmet. Huddy, who has arrived by car well before me, feels my pulse, diagnoses accumulated fatigue, and prescribes rest. But it is too late, as by that stage I am fast asleep.

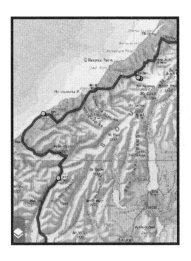

DAY 21

NO ORTHOPAEDIC SURGEONS (OR PLASTIC ONES) AT LAKE PARINGA
Franz Josef to Haast – 163 km

To get from Franz Josef to Fox Glacier, a distance of a mere 30 km, I have to haul Spot over three murderously steep saddles – 321 m, 408 m and 411 m high. It is hard work; my left knee does not like it one bit and goes on strike.

'C'mon, knee, give me a hand here,' I plead.

But my knee shakes his head, closes his eyes and crosses his arms over his chest, not willing to discuss the matter any further.

I arrive in the Fox Glacier township two hours later. I have a coffee with Dutch apple cake and a handful of painkillers.

I think back to the message I received from my little sister, who lives in the Netherlands and who follows my daily blog with some

Day 21: Looking towards Franz Josef Glacier.

concern. It finishes with the quote: 'Listen to the whisper of your body so it does not have to scream.' I mull this over and conclude, 'Fat lot of good that will do me. That quote will definitely not get me to Bluff. I might as well lie down and die now.' I lock the quote in that part of my brain where I keep quotes which are not suitable for the situation I find myself in at the time but which might come in handy at a later date. I will save this one for when I am on my deathbed and my body and mind whisper that my time is up and a doctor will come and help me out before my body and mind start screaming. I decide that the 'whisper quote' is an excellent argument for euthanasia. I will email Princess Jacinda, as the government is currently discussing a proposed euthanasia bill. It can be called the 'Whisper Bill'. I search my brain to find a more appropriate quote for my current dilemma. Hidden in a dark corner I find: 'Pain is temporary; quitting lasts forever.' Lance Armstrong mentioned this in a television interview. I consider the since-disgraced bike rider who beat cancer and who won five fake Tour de France victories one of life's great disappointments, but the quote stuck and suits its purpose today.

The road to Fox Glacier is closed due to damage from the same cyclone which had made life difficult for me on Day 11. I find a swing bridge from where I can look up the glacier valley, with the summit of Mount Cook just visible, towering majestically in the distance. It is a stunning view and with the swing bridge gently swaying under my feet it feels that time is standing still for a moment. From Fox Glacier

Day 21: View from the swing bridge with Mount Cook just visible in the distance.

township there is quite a bit of downhill, which gives my bothersome knee a rest and my brain the opportunity to contemplate some more.

I had emailed my mate Pete in Christchurch to ask him what I can do about my bum and knee issues. Pete knows a lot about cycling and everything that comes with it. This is what he came up with:

1)   Get a round seat.
2)   Put ice on your backside at the end of the day when you come off the bike.
3)   Check that your pedal is not bent.

I am now contemplating this advice and decide that it is as useless as a chocolate teapot. First of all, I have only seen round seats on women's bikes, and when the other Tour riders see me use a women's seat they will think I have gone soft – which I have, but I don't want to make it so bleeding obvious. Spot is unlikely to take kindly to the suggestion either, as it will turn him into a transgender bike. There is nothing wrong with transgenderism, but Spot would need to give his consent, and I guess that he is not in the mood for something so drastic. Furthermore, I can't think of anything worse than putting ice on my butt. Imagine it! I shiver at the thought. And why my pedal would be bent is beyond me, let alone knowing what to do about it if it is. I could kick it is the best I can come up with, but my foot would probably come off second best, only to result in another ailment to be added to the list.

To lift my mood, I steer my contemplations from problems to solutions, and I come up with a brilliant idea. My destination that day is the Lake Paringa Lodge, located on the shores of . . . well, would you believe it . . . Lake Paringa. I will visit an orthopaedic and a plastic surgeon on my arrival for a knee replacement and a butt implant. Voilà, two foolproof solutions for my main two ailments, just like that. Brilliant!

But when I arrive at the lake, I can't find an orthopaedic surgeon anywhere, and neither can I find a plastic one. Instead, I meet plenty of sandflies the size of bumblebees. I thought I had seen it all at Lake Rotoroa, but these critters are a different kettle of fish (or is it 'cattle of fish'? No, as cows are cattle and fish are fish).

Just then I remember the favourable tailwind which has accompanied me all day and I decide to carry on and leave Lake Paringa behind.

I have had it with this lake, its sandflies and the lack of orthopaedic and plastic surgeons. My sore knee feels much better. It must have got a fright when he heard that he was going to be replaced.

Day 21: Bruce Bay, where I met up again with Paul.

My mind wanders back to 'a kettle of fish'. I can understand a kettle of sandflies, which I would happily turn on to boil them alive. I contemplate whether I would do the same if the kettle contained fish. But decide probably not, and I wonder why that is. What is the difference between a kettle of sandflies and a kettle of fish? Then I know the answer. The sandflies attack you all the time, for no reason, except that they are hungry. They have no mercy and you can't reason with them. This means that if you have the chance, you should retaliate, and what better way than boiling them in a kettle. Fish, in contrast, wish us no harm, except for the great white shark, but they do not fit in the kettle anyway, so I decide to leave the great white out of this discussion. I decide that I will let the fish in the kettle live, unless I am starving from hunger. In that case it will be me or the fish, so I would have no choice. Still, boiling them alive seems cruel, as cruel as putting a fishhook through their mouth. I come up with a solution. I will stick an electric cable into a power point at one end and dangle the other in the kettle. This will kill the fish so quickly that their small brains will not realise what has happened until they are already dead. But I am still not happy with this solution. I hope never to be put in this predicament and decide to drop the topic.

At Bruce Bay, I meet up with my friend Paul from security who had guided me into Wellington on Day 13. Once again we team up.

With the tailwind not slacking, we make good time and arrive in Haast in the early evening.

Huddy welcomes us at a holiday house he has booked at short notice. Not only that, he also cooks us all a wholesome meal.

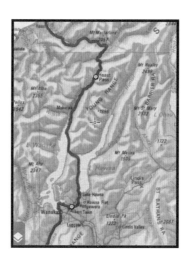

DAY 22

FIRST YOU SUFFER, THEN YOU DIE
Haast to Wānaka – 152 km

I wake up the next morning to a steady drizzle outside, expected to worsen during the day. I set off early on the Haast Pass–Makarora Road with Wānaka as my destination. Paul is still fast asleep.

I have left Haast well behind when the rain turns to a downpour as if all toilet flushes in heaven are jammed at once. I have never experienced rain this heavy, not even on my wettest day in the North Island. I am fully dressed in protective gear, including my special rain hat, but the rain goes straight through my jacket, hat and pants and my feet are squelching in my shoes.

Despite the wet, I get very hot, as the road towards Haast Pass climbs gradually. The perspiration from my skin has nowhere to go, which increases the wetness of my three layers of clothing even more.

The Haast Pass climb starts properly 50 km into the ride, indicated by a sudden increase in steepness which forces me to change into Spot's lowest gear. Haast Pass might not be the highest in New Zealand, but at 564 metres it is definitely the steepest, I reckon. While grinding up the hill, I am confronted by waterfalls which come thundering down from the rocky slope beside the road with such force that I get sprayed with wetness even more. Not that it matters, as I can't get any wetter. I might as well bike in my Speedos. Except that I am now getting cold, as the temperature has dropped to single figures as I approach the summit of the pass. Suddenly, on the side of the road, a lone figure appears out of the thick rain. It is Huddy, hidden behind layers of waterproof jackets, hats and pants. 'Come on,' he shouts. 'You can do it!' To which I cry out, 'First you suffer, then you die.'

Huddy gives me an encouraging grin before he flees back to the safety of his car. The weather gods must have overheard me. They don't

Day 22: Waterfalls reach the road.   *First you suffer, then you die.*

want me to die (yet), so the rain eases as I approach Makarora. I arrive at the Makarora café feeling and looking like I have just survived a drowning.

In the café, I spot Huddy looking comfortable behind a double-shot flat white, engrossed in his newspaper. I sneak up behind him and stand there for a moment, still dripping heavily from all parts of my body before letting out a loud 'boo'. Huddy gets such a fright that he jumps a metre high. When he recovers, we both have a good laugh. I find another friend in the café by the name of John Walker who lives in Wānaka and offers to accompany me there. Before you ask, no, it is not 'the' John Walker; he does not run fast enough for that.

I change into some dry clothes, have a feed of chicken pie and chips, wash it down with a milkshake, and feel much better. Huddy and I say an emotional farewell, as we will not see each other again till Bluff; that is, if I make it that far. Hauling Spot and his load up the Haast Pass in

Day 22: Tailwind helping along the top reaches of Lake Wānaka.

the cold and wet has caused my back to 'go out' and my lower spine is now gradually tightening up. I can only sit on my bike in one position: half upright and slightly skewed to one side. Every little movement or bump in the road causes a stabbing pain in my lower back, like I am being poked with a hot iron. At least it is dry and we have a decent westerly tailwind. John Walker is a bit of a chatterbox (ex-lawyer . . .). I listen with half an ear (as using both ears would be a bit much), but it is pleasant enough.

Suddenly my front tyre loses pressure and goes down fast.

'Bugger. A flattie,' I call out to my companion.

We stop and replace the inner tube of the tyre without too much trouble. Twenty minutes later, the same tyre deflates for a second time. This second puncture is more serious, as I have no more spare tubes and no repair kit, as that is still with Huddy – the one and most important item I forgot to take over from him when he left the Tour

Day 22: The cycle trail along the Hāwea River.

on that fateful day. John Walker has an old mountain-bike with 26-inch wheels; Spot's wheels are 29-inch, so that is not going to work either. I think about solutions, as I have learned that for most problems there is a solution, but only if you stay calm and think. I could walk, or keep pumping the tyre up while I am riding (although that would be difficult to achieve and has probably never been done before). We could call for help, except that we have no cell-phone coverage where we are. What to do?

We muck about with the two flat inner tubes, pumping them up repeatedly as if the tyre would get sick of it and decide to close the hole themselves and keep the air in just to get a break from all the pumping. The time passes slowly. We are at a loss what to do when the solution arrives in the form of Paul from security. He is carrying a repair kit (of course).

I quickly fix the leak following the instructions from Paul, as it has been a long time since I have patched a leaking tyre – roadies tend to just replace them. On our way we go, turning off at Hāwea to follow the cycling trails of the Hāwea and Clutha rivers till we reach the home of John Walker in the early evening. Paul wants to get to Cardrona that night and carries on. Heather, John's better half, has cooked a wonderful meal for us, with salmon as the main dish (I manage to avoid any thoughts as to how it was caught) and ice cream and strawberries for dessert.

CONQUERING THE CROWN RANGE
Wānaka to Queenstown – 95 km

It is still dark outside when I wake up the next morning. I make myself a strong coffee, do some administration and check the weather forecast; today is still favourable but it will turn to custard, or shit, or whatever you want to call it, the day after. I prefer custard over shit – I like custard but I have also learned that as far as the weather is concerned, custard and shit are pretty much the same thing.

Tomorrow, on Day 24, I will have to tackle one of the more difficult routes of the Tour: 103 km of gravel roads and bike trails between Walter Peak Station and Mossburn, with the 600-metre-high Von Hill smack bang in the middle. Walter Peak Station is located across Lake Wakatipu and can only be reached from Queenstown by boat. Tour riders are advised to take the tourist steamship the TSS *Earnslaw*, which should have been called the 'Earn-slow', as it is not particularly speedy. The *Earnslaw* does not arrive at Walter Peak Station till late morning, which means that even on a good day it will be a tight deadline to get to Mossburn before dark. The predicted change to a southerly means that the wind will blow straight from Antarctica, across the Southern Ocean, into the Von Valley and into my face. The southerly headwind will be accompanied by rain, cold, sleet and snow. I have a healthy respect for cold, as I do not carry much body fat to protect me.

I should be able get to Queenstown today, but what then? I call my friend Morg for advice. Morg lives in the foothills of Arthurs Point near Queenstown. I can't always get hold of him because he spends a lot of time outside cell-phone range, but this time I do. That is lucky. Even luckier is that Morg has a little jet boat, and when he hears about my predicament, he offers to take me across Lake Wakatipu with his jet boat early the next morning. That way I can stay ahead

Day 23: Cardrona Hotel, a coffee stop before the Crown Range.

of the weather change for as long as possible, as the southerly is not expected to hit until midday.

Before I leave the home of Heather and John, I get a call from a mate from Christchurch who goes by the nickname Grey Weka. He is in Wānaka for a holiday and keen to accompany me for part of the day's ride. We meet at the foreshore of Lake Wānaka to ride up the Cardrona Valley and Crown Range together. Grey Weka suggests that I draft behind him for the ride. That idea appeals to me. The road gradually rises for the first 24 km to the Cardrona Hotel, where we will stop for a coffee before tackling the Crown Range Pass, the highest point of the Tour at just over 1000 metres.

But riding up the valley, I find myself leading, with Grey Weka in my wake. We have a good chat, but Grey Weka refuses to take over the lead as promised. I am too polite to point this out (which is unlike me), but I enjoy the company. I conclude that Grey Weka has turned up just to get his name into this story. Or, maybe that might be a bit harsh; perhaps Grey Weka has come along to make sure that I am doing okay, or for some other mysterious reason. Grey Weka is known to be a bit of an enigma. I decide to leave it at that.

When we have coffee at the Cardrona Hotel, Grey Weka suddenly announces that he needs to head back to Wānaka. He explains that his wife is waiting for him. She is called Rose. Just from her name you can read that she must be beautiful, so I do not blame him and get ready to tackle the Crown Range alone. I have done the climb a number of times when I was younger and I am looking forward to it, but expectation is the mother of all crises and when the climb starts in earnest, I realise that I have never done it on a heavily laden mountain-bike and with a malfunctioning back. Ever so slowly I grind my way up the steep road, sitting skew-whiff on the bike, unable to change position or stand up on the pedals for extra power.

On the Queenstown side of the Crown Range, the course instructions direct me onto bike trails. The scenery is stunning and I try to take it all in, but I also have to look carefully underfoot, or, rather, underwheel, as the gravel, stones and rocks I encounter try to throw me off-balance. Also my lower back is screaming out by now.

I arrive at Morg's place early in the evening in a state of exhaustion and disrepair. Morg suggests we have dinner in Queenstown. I am not even hungry but too tired to protest. I grin my way through a painful 90 minutes sitting on a hard chair at the Lone Star munching on some spare ribs while Morg updates me about his latest adventures. He is a bit of a speed devil. Going fast is his passion, be it jet boating, downhill mountain biking or riding his motorbike. Morg has his own private orthopaedic surgeon who puts him back together again after his inevitable speed-related crashes. Morg, I know, will never change his ways.

Day 23: Crown Range Summit, the highest point of the Tour.

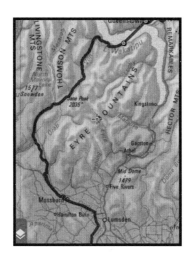

DAY 24

MISERY IN ITS PUREST FORM
Queenstown to Mossburn – 103 km

At 4 am I struggle to get up, not because of the early hour but because my back does not let me. Every little movement feels like I am being whacked in my lower back by a thousand jackhammers. I know from experience that I have to be patient and take it easy for a few days, but that won't get me to Bluff. Me and my back have developed a delicate relationship over the years, with mutual tolerance and understanding. I explain to my back that I have two more days to go and after that I will give him plenty of rest. My back responds by locking up completely, which causes such pain that it takes my breath away. I have to lie very still for a while till the pain eases a fraction.

Finally, I manage to haul myself out of bed. I know the pain will get better if I keep moving gently. But when I try to put my socks on, my back simply does not allow it. I am determined not to ask Morg to help, as that would be humiliating. At the worst of times, when this has happened in the past, I let Ien put my socks on. But Morg? No way! I lie on my back and rock gently backwards and forwards while trying to hook my big toe into the opening of my sock. Twenty agonising minutes later both feet are covered. The socks are on crooked but I do not care, as they will soon be hidden by my shoes. Trying to put *them* on turns into another battle. By the time I have completed the task I am exhausted, and the day has not even started.

Morg has his boat locked and loaded on a trailer that's hooked onto the back of his van. When we arrive at the shore of Lake Wakatipu at 5 am for the trip across to Walter Peak Station, it is still pitch-dark. Morg launches the boat, with Spot strapped onto the rear deck. I am pretty useless in helping because of my back but also because of my general uselessness when assisting others with anything mechanical.

Day 24: Spot on Morg's boat – ready to launch.

Morg's boat is not only tiny but it is also battered, with lots of dents, bumps and scratches, evidence of the twirly-whirlies these boats are famous for when trying to avoid rocks and low-hanging tree branches in narrow gorges with openings so small you couldn't even squeeze your grandmother through. If you saw it, you would think it is the cutest little jet boat in the world, but if you are in it, that perception changes rapidly. Morg gives me a set of earmuffs to prevent noise-induced deafness. In jet boating, the noisier the motor, the faster the boat, and this little cutie makes a hell of a racket.

Morg pushes the boat off, jumps in and starts the motor. 'Ke-doink,' the motor says, and goes silent. Morg turns the key again and the same thing happens.

'This does not sound good,' I think.

Morg utters the f-word, which is unusual for him, so that gets me worried even more. We row the little boat back to shore by using our

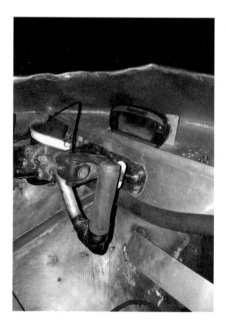 

Day 24: The jet-boat cockpit.   *Engine trouble is soon fixed.*

hands as paddles. Luckily Morg is very smart. He can take a motor apart and put it back together again in no time; any motor – a car, motorbike, boat or even a weed eater. I would take a lifetime to take a motor apart and I would need more than another lifetime to put it back together again.

Morg bangs away at the motor in a frenzy using a range of different tools. After 15 minutes, eureka, the motor explodes into life, confirming Morg's reputation as a mechanical genius.

Off we go at a hundred miles an hour, with the boat going bumpity-bumpity-bump on the early-morning ripples of the lake. The jarring causes my back to go into an acute spasm. I am in agony and plead with Morg to slow down, but Morg has earmuffs on his balding head and a big grin on his face. He misunderstands me, thinking that I want to go faster, and opens the throttle even further. In desperation, I throw myself at Morg and stick my down-turned thumb in front of his face.

Day 24: Morg in action.

The tiniest boat in the world in all its glory.

Morg gets the message and continues at a more sedate pace. The trip takes all of a few minutes.

The TSS *Earnslaw* is still fast asleep at the jetty in Queenstown when I stand on the pebbled beach at Walter Peak Station under a brightening sky, waving goodbye to Morg. Too late, I discover that I still have my life jacket on.

I consider keeping it on as it might be handy when the southerly hits. It will keep me warm or even afloat if necessary.

Just when I turn my back to the lake to get going, the roar of the jet boat comes back to within earshot. Morg is returning to recover the missing life jacket. On arrival, he does a huge twirly just before he hits the beach, soaking me from head to toe.

I set off in a light southerly breeze – the quiet before the storm. The scenery is stunning. Fragments of low-hanging clouds cover sections of mountain slopes. Distant snowy peaks are visible, mirrored perfectly in the crystal-clear lake. I feel the cold and stomp hard on the pedals in an attempt to warm up. My back and knee are competing for attention. I want to enjoy this part of the ride, as I know that soon it will become ugly. After a while, I am caught up by a woman and a male rider who have also taken an early-morning private water taxi. We do some introductions and ask the usual questions, 'where are you from' and 'why are you here'. The woman volunteers that she has five kids and that the Tour is her excuse to get some peace for a while. 'Anything to get out of the house,' she says. They are both strong riders, and normally I would have let them go, but this time I decide to stick with them for as long as possible, as I would like some company for when the southerly arrives and the going gets tough.

Just when we reach the summit of Von Hill, the storm hits us front on. From one moment to the next we are surrounded by black, wet and wind so forceful that, bent over our handlebars, we need all our

Day 24: Lake Wakatipu, the calm before the storm.

Day 24: Mossburn Railway Hotel – we arrived there soaked and frozen.

strength to keep moving forward. When we look up momentarily to see where we are going, our faces are cut to pieces by the hail and sleet. The temperature has dropped to freezing point. We are only 30 km into the ride and still have 70 km to go, mostly on gravel roads which soon turn into mud.

Once over the top of the hill, much of the road runs gradually downhill, but that is well and truly compensated for by the headwind, snow, sleet and the tyre-sucking mud. The icy wind and sleet do not let up, and despite working hard, we are feeling the cold. Our hands and feet go numb and our faces sting. We know that we have to keep going; it is the only way to survive, as there is nowhere to shelter.

There is not much talking. Loss of feeling in our fingers makes it difficult to use the gear levers and brakes. I am in a cocoon of misery in its purest form. 'The second-to-last day and this happens. Bloody well my luck,' I mutter to myself, but I am grateful for the company of the other two, as shared suffering is easier to endure.

We arrive at the Mossburn Railway Hotel at the fall of darkness. We heave our shivering bodies off our bikes and defrost in front of a big wood fire in the lounge of the hotel. I realise that today has been a closely fought thing, perhaps the closest I have been to perishing during the whole of this tour. I am grateful that I, my back and my knee have survived the day.

As soon as I put my tired head down on the pillow, I hear the gravel-grinding sound of a boisterous snorer. It is loud and persistent. I bonk on the wall with my fist, but the snoring becomes even louder. I put my earplugs in but can still hear the noise. I put my pillow over my head rather than under it, but that does not help much either, as I can still feel the vibrations travelling through my body.

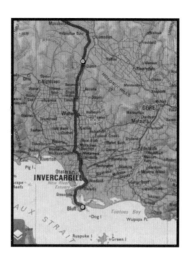

DAY 25

ALL'S WELL THAT ENDS WELL
Mossburn to Bluff – 137 km

I must have fallen asleep at some stage, as when I wake at 5 am with a searing headache and with the snoring next door still in full swing, I remember a bad dream about chainsaws. I get up, make myself a strong coffee, do some administration, have breakfast and get ready to hit the road one last time. It is still semi-dark, bitterly cold, with a steady drizzle to keep me company. I have four layers of clothing on, including three lots of cycling pants, gloves, a balaclava and my helmet cover.

Despite the layers of clothing, within no time I am frozen stiff. I stop, swing my arms around and stamp my feet to get the blood flowing before continuing. The drizzle slowly eases, patches of blue sky appear overhead, the temperature goes up from zero to a more tolerable level and the feeling gradually returns to my hands and feet.

There is a slight headwind. Best of all is that there are mainly sealed roads and no hills anywhere to be seen. This is serious aerobar country. I like to use my aerobars when I can, and today I will use them all day.

Just before midday I reach Winton, the halfway mark. I stop and have bacon and eggs on toast. Huddy makes a surprise appearance and joins me for the final 60 km stretch to Bluff. This makes me very happy, as we had started together and now we are going to finish together. Something went wrong somewhere in between but that doesn't matter any more now.

I let Huddy lead the way, as I suddenly feel dog-tired. I fantasise that there will be a huge crowd waiting at the finish line. I will be interviewed by the assembled press, have my picture taken with all and sundry, sign hundreds of autographs and receive congratulatory calls from Princess Jacinda and the Queen.

In reality, the welcoming party at Stirling Point, south of Bluff, consists of a crowd of one. Helene has been waiting patiently for hours in the freezing wind, which never leaves this southernmost part of the mainland. It is an emotional time for us all. We have shared much these last few weeks. Things did not go according to plan, but they seldom do. So you adjust, and that we did, the best we could.

Spot is quietly observing proceedings and does not join in the celebrations, as bikes have little emotion. Spot is of course the real hero of the story. He never missed a beat except for the day that he allowed his front tyre to go down. Bar that incident Spot has been as loyal and reliable as a Trump supporter for the remainder of the Tour.

'Let's bike back to Christchurch,' I suggest to Huddy with a serious voice.

Huddy's eyes grow twice their normal size and his face turns pale. Then he realises that I am having him on, as he knows full well that my physical and mental state will not allow me to do one more pedal stroke.

Day 25: We started together and finished together.

TIPS

In the unlikely event, after reading this story, you still want to do the Tour Aotearoa, I have jotted down some random tips:

A mountain-bike travels much slower than a road bike.

Every day takes longer than you think, even if when the weather is in your favour.

Be prepared for adverse weather conditions in the form of head-winds, rain and cold. They can arrive at any time on any day, individually or as a team. Consider a nice weather day as a bonus.

Plan your trip carefully; seek advice from the Tour Aotearoa website (www.touraotearoa.nz), the Tour Aotearoa guidebooks and experienced bike packers.

If you are a novice bike packer, avoid the Grade 4 and 5 mountain-bike trails, which are the Kaiwhakauka Track on the North Island and the Maungatapu and Waiuta (Big River) tracks on the South Island. When the guidebook says things like 'This trail is not suitable for heavily laden mountain-bikes', then it means that the trail is not suitable for heavily laden mountain-bikes! If you are an optimist and still want to do these trails, make sure you are with more experienced riders who know what they are doing and where they are going. Alternative routes are available; be grateful for that. I was. Rename 'chicken' routes to 'wise' routes to make them more appealing.

Have a plan but be prepared to adjust your plan from day to day. Book accommodation in advance, but don't kill yourself to try to get there if you are having a bad day. It is better to lose the odd deposit. In the bigger scheme of the journey, it is not important.

Tour Aotearoa has more hills than you can shake a stick at. Every time you think, 'Surely this will be the last one for the day', there is guaranteed to be at least one more. The only day with no hills is the final day into Bluff, although the prevailing southerly wind in that part of the country can well and truly make up for that.

Tents or bivvy bags are carried by the hard-out bike packers. It is not essential, as there is a surprising number and variety of accommodation options available along the way.

One of the better recovery drinks is chocolate milk.

Get specialised bike-packing bags (e.g. from www.robo-kiwi.co.nz, Kiwi made). They can be attached to the seat, just below the handlebars, and/or in between the triangle of the frame. They are attached to the bike in such a way that it is not only shake-proof but also optimally balanced. I had a carrier on the front which came crashing down onto my front wheel on Day 3. The carrier on the back was free floating, attached to the seat post, with a heavy bag clipped on top. This worked well on the smoother surfaces but bounced around on the rough. It is a miracle, or just good engineering, that the carrier did not break at some stage on the rougher trails.

The instructions in the course book are generally good to follow, but a GPS is handy for when you get lost and when navigating through Auckland. Make sure that you know how a GPS works. For some people, like me, this is not a given. It also helps to be multilingual, as sometimes the GPS speaks a different language.

It is not a good idea to carry a laptop.

Some sense of planning and urgency is required if you want to do the route within the required 30 days, but try to maintain a sense of harmony, equilibrium and humour.

Be mindful of a unique experience; take it in as much as possible. The scenery is awesome.

Contemplation can be a useful and satisfying distraction . . . often.

ACKNOWLEDGMENTS
AND A FINAL CONTEMPLATION

Thanks go to my family and friends for their comments, support and encouragement during the Tour. Without that, it is unlikely that I would have made it to Bluff. I can't mention every individual family member and friend by name, but I want to make an exception for John and Helene Hudson and of course Ien. They came to meet me several times during the Tour to accompany me, comfort me and feed me. Huddy went well beyond his duty providing ongoing support and encouragement following his forced withdrawal from the Tour. They embody the saying that, in the end, all that is left is family and friends.

I want to thank Marja Slack for the first 'deep edit' of this manuscript. Having English as a second language is a frustration I have learned to live with.

Thanks also to Warren Adler, Kevin Chapman and their colleagues at Upstart Press who were fantastic to work with. They left my experience of the Tour intact, improved the layout and added colour with the strategic placement of photos I took during my adventure.

The kindness I have encountered during my trip is incredible, not only from friends and family but also from total strangers and other riders en route. It has confirmed my belief that we live in a special country. The uniqueness of the Kiwi culture is not limited to the courage expressed on the battlefields and when playing sport. The united response of the majority of the population to the 2011 Christchurch earthquake, the mosque shooting in 2019 and the current Covid-19 pandemic is proof that toughness and kindness are not mutually exclusive.

After this final contemplation, I want to say one more thank you, and that is to the Kennett brothers, the lions of New Zealand mountain biking, for putting on this epic biennial event in true Kiwi spirit, with wisdom, kindness and humour.

TOUR AOTEAROA – 2018: AT A GLANCE

- 660 entrants – 525 starters, of which 457 finished at Bluff.
- 22% women, 78% men.
- Time: 10–31 days (average 23 days).
- Age: women 10–70, men 23–76 years.
- Kiwi riders are older than overseas riders.
- Bikes: 80% mountain-bikes, 10% specialist bike-packing bikes. Not sure what type of bike the remaining 10% used.
- Older riders take longer and camp less (56 riders didn't camp once, including the author).
- Total elevation of the tour is 35 km – four times the height of Mount Everest.
- Funds raised for charity by the event: $300,000, including $60,000 used for track upgrades.
- Many ride the Tour route outside the official event, between September and April. Sensibly, most tend to take their time, from two to three months.

(Information provided by Jonathan Kennett)